To Joan,
Happy Birthday

SNOW ON THE LINDIS

With love,
Jack

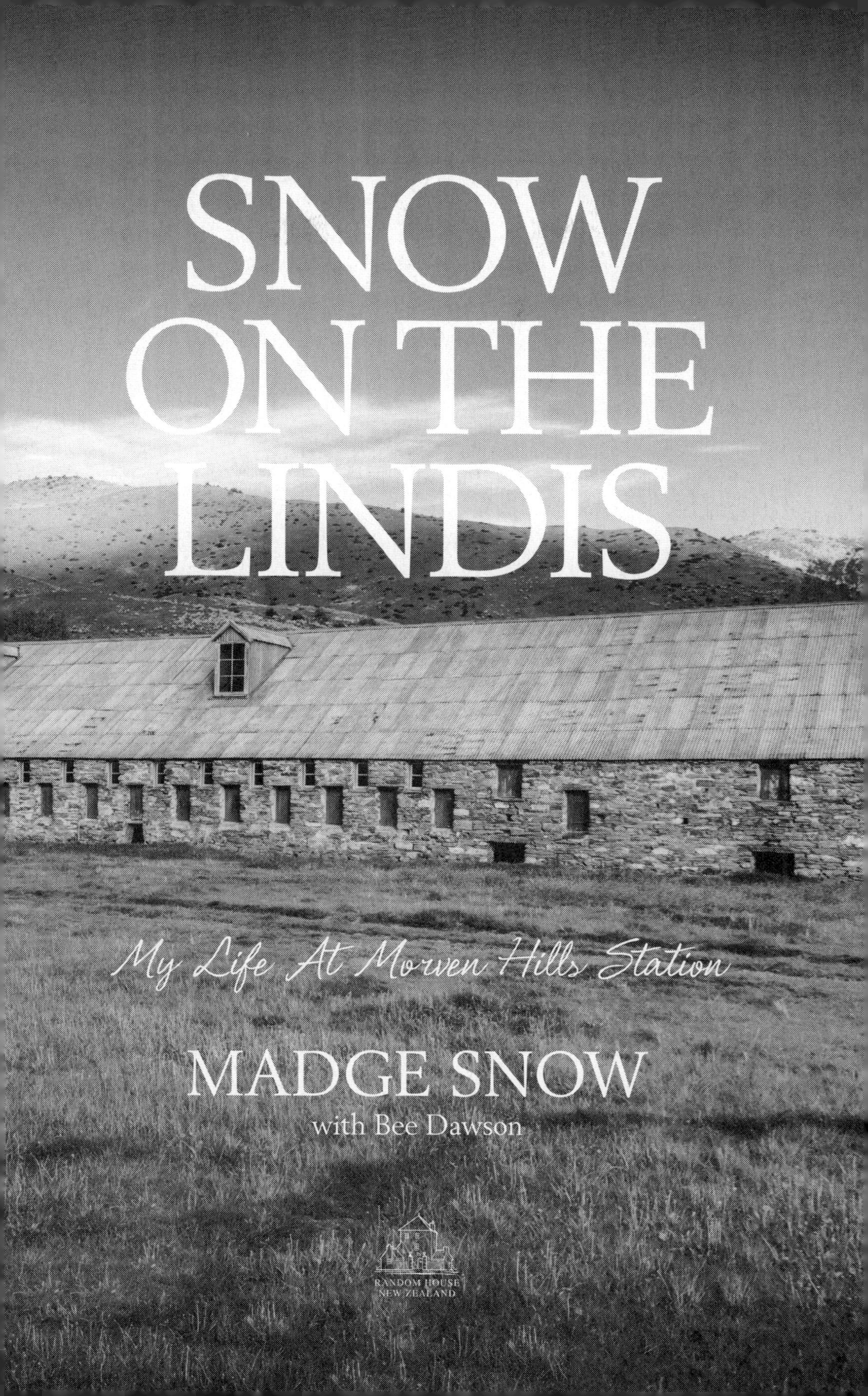

SNOW ON THE LINDIS

My Life At Morven Hills Station

MADGE SNOW

with Bee Dawson

RANDOM HOUSE
NEW ZEALAND

Part of the royalties from the sale of this book will go to the Otago Brain Injury Association

RANDOM HOUSE

UK | USA | Canada | Ireland | Australia
India | New Zealand | South Africa | China

Random House is an imprint of the Penguin Random House group of companies, whose addresses can be found at global.penguinrandomhouse.com.

Penguin Random House New Zealand

First published by Penguin Random House New Zealand, 2015

1 3 5 7 9 10 8 6 4 2

Design by Carla Sy © Penguin Random House New Zealand
Cover photographs by Ruth Brown (back cover and front top) and Todd and Sarah Sisson, Lighthouse Media Limited (front bottom)
Printed and bound in Australia by Griffin Press, an Accredited ISO AS/NZS 14001 Environmental Management Systems Printer
A catalogue record for this book is available from the National Library of New Zealand.

ISBN 978-1-77553-792-2
eISBN 978-1-77553-793-9

penguinrandomhouse.co.nz

I dedicate this book

to my father
whose assessment and vision
established the dream

to my mother
who worked so hard to keep the dream alive

and to my wonderful family
who all share in it.

This lovely building has a dignity
in keeping with its vast size . . .

Contents

The 34-stand woolshed

Introduction

It was late afternoon when we drove over the Lindis. The landscape was incredibly beautiful — a special part of Otago. Wind rippled the tussocks. They were a warm caramel colour with a wonderful silky sheen.

UNDULATING ACROSS THE VALLEY were a series of gentle breast-like mounds. It was as though God had reached out with a giant flour sifter and given the sides a gentle tap. Baby hills which had abandoned all hope of becoming mountains. We stopped on the top and stretched our legs. There was an eerie silence; a lone hawk drawing circles in the sky and the dominant feeling of space. We filled our lungs with the pure clean air and, after a quick kiss, marvelled at how lucky we were. A surge of honeymoon happiness welled in my heart; Morven Hills was just down the road.

Max was overflowing with impatience, he was anxious to keep moving. After all, he told me, he hadn't seen his dogs for over two weeks. On 14 March 1954, just 17 days into our marriage, I knew I had competition.

Fifteen kilometres down the pass we turned off the main road and drove through the red gates. The air was filled with white fluff, a world of candy floss. It looked like thistledown but Max told me it was cotton from the black poplars. As I shut the gate I scooped up a handful but, despite there being no wind, its gossamer fluff floated airily away.

Racing down the drive came two dogs. They'd recognised the car, and were wildly excited. 'There's Peg and Toss!' Max's voice showed his excitement. When we pulled up in front of an old white-washed house, an elderly man was leaning on the gate. He had a big felt hat down round his ears and I thought he was going to raise it, but no — he was lifting his arm to yell at the animals. 'Bloody hell, them dogs thought yoose never coming back,' he addressed Max. Peg was half in the car and Toss was christening the front tyre.

A big man, George Martin gave the impression that he somehow overflowed in several directions at once; he was 70 years old, florid, and wore a wide-brimmed hat and brown tweed trousers over the top of pink long johns. The pink was folded over five centimetres and everything was held up by sturdy braces. To complete the picture, he wore a pink short-sleeved woollen singlet. You could say he was a colourful character. As long as I knew George I never saw him dressed any other way.

'Bloody hell, yoose be the new missus,' he said, crunching my hand. 'I've got the fire stoked up for yoose. An' the kettle's a-boiling if you wanna cup o' tea.' George followed us into the kitchen and sat on the seat under the window. There was a wooden table and four rickety chairs, but taking centre stage was a black and red Shacklock range. 'Bloody hell; Dirty Dora, that's what I call her. Yoose call her what you like.' By this stage the well-stoked Dora was almost red hot, the kettle was jumping up and down and splattering everywhere, the overheated cistern was giving off a deep-throated rumble,

the dogs were barking and George was talking non-stop. A cacophony of sound waiting on the maestro to raise his baton. With a flourish George picked up his polished walnut-coloured manuka stick, waved it baton-like in the air, and said, 'I'll see yoose tomorrow.'

Well, I thought. Let the show begin!

Some of the kennels

"... inspired by men who
knew and loved stone"

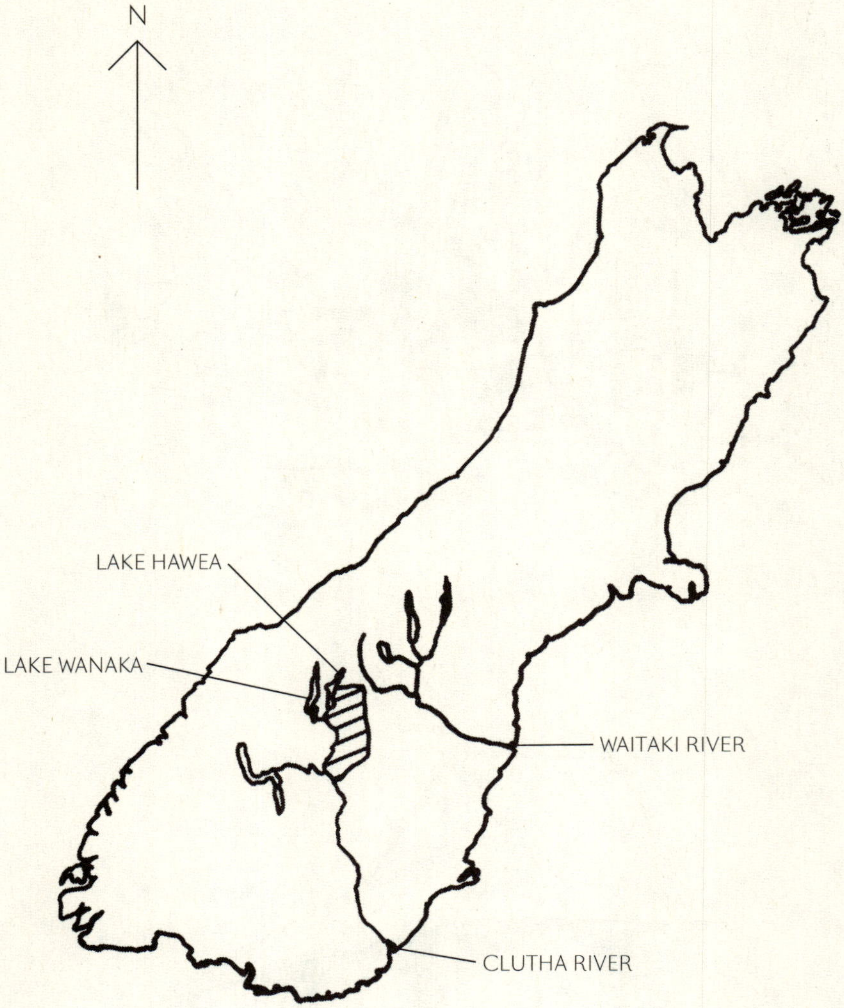

MORVEN HILLS STATION PRIOR TO BEING SUBDIVIDED IN 1910

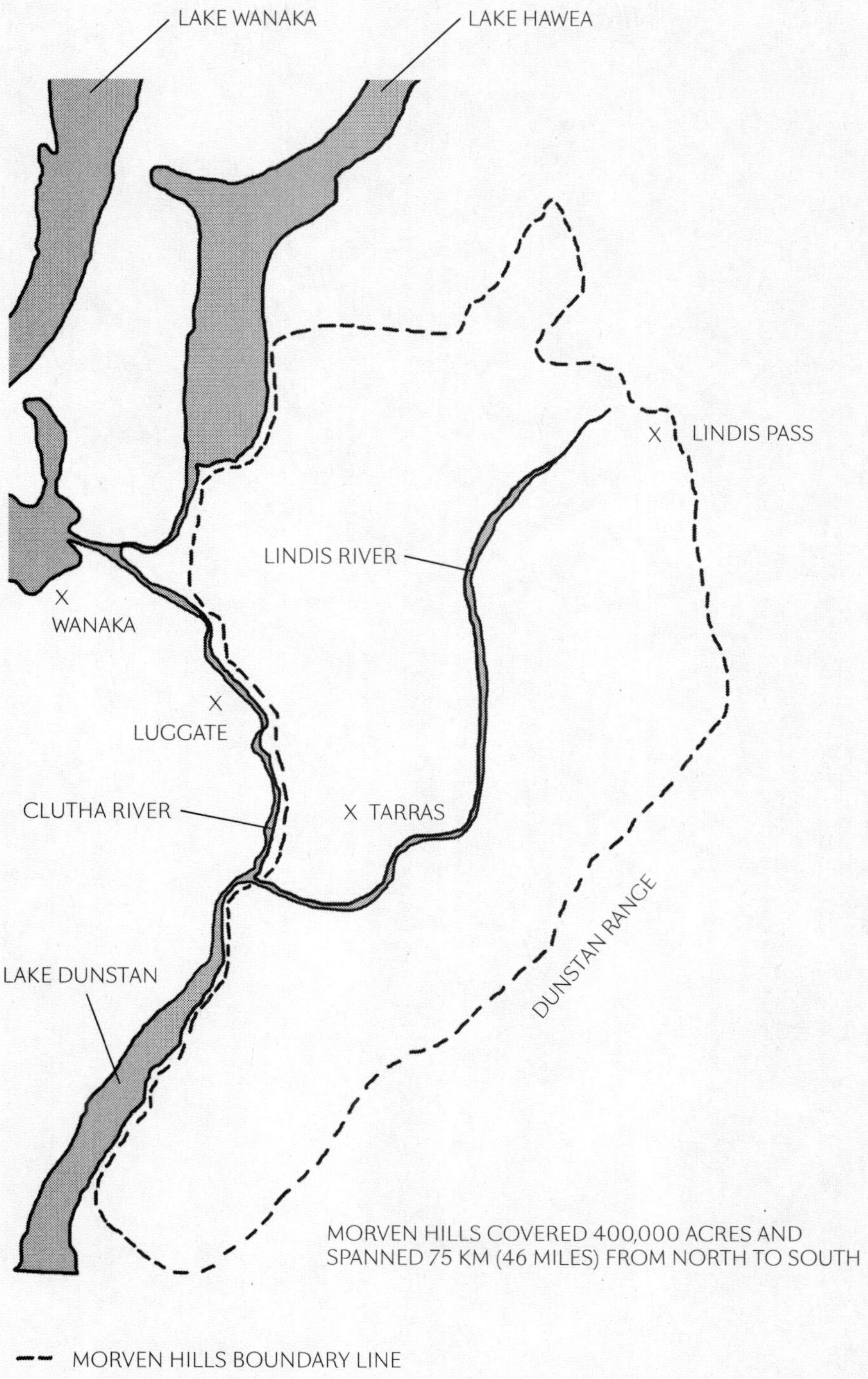
LAKE WANAKA
LAKE HAWEA
LINDIS PASS
LINDIS RIVER
WANAKA
LUGGATE
CLUTHA RIVER
TARRAS
DUNSTAN RANGE
LAKE DUNSTAN
MORVEN HILLS COVERED 400,000 ACRES AND SPANNED 75 KM (46 MILES) FROM NORTH TO SOUTH
MORVEN HILLS BOUNDARY LINE

BLACK

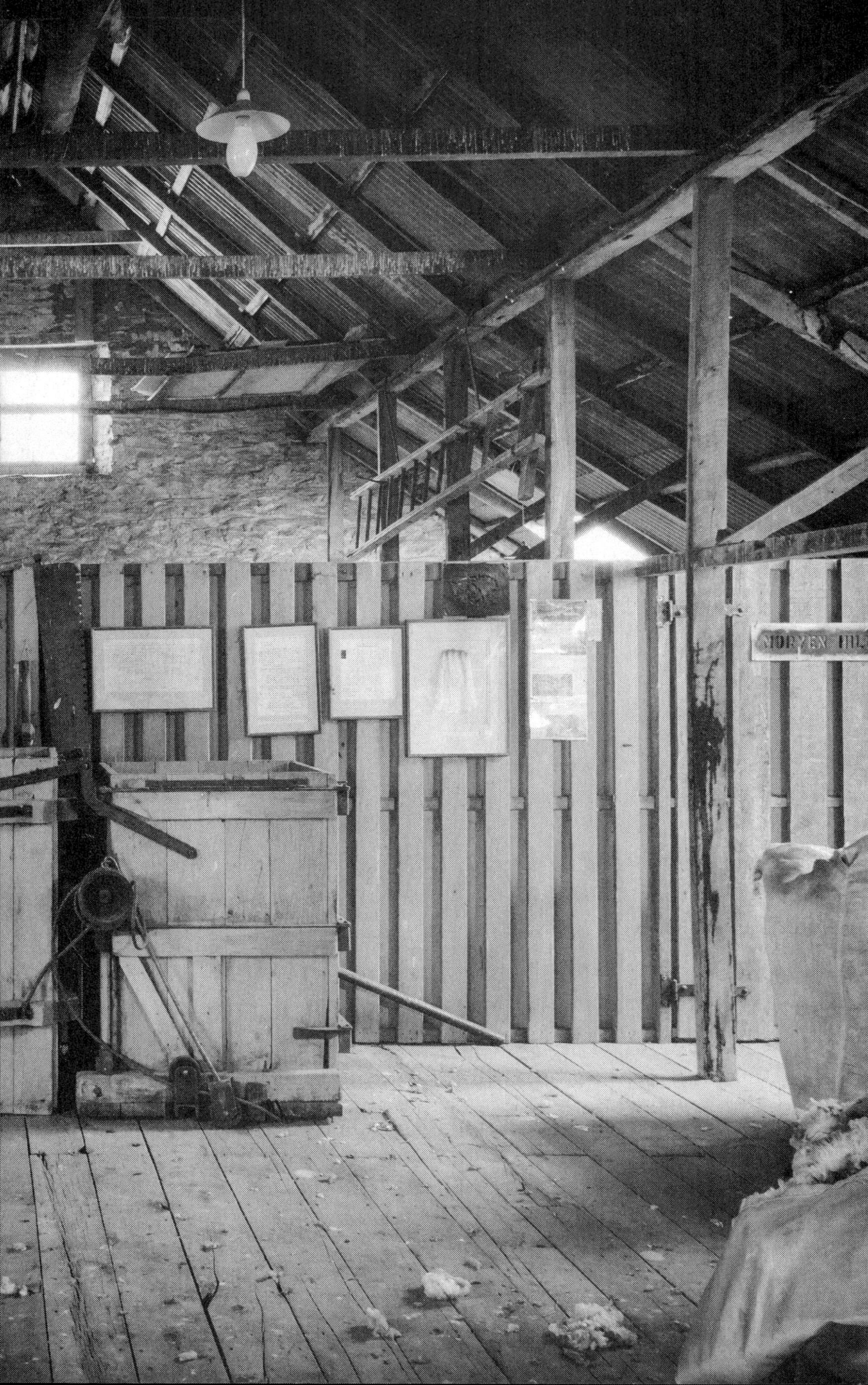

34

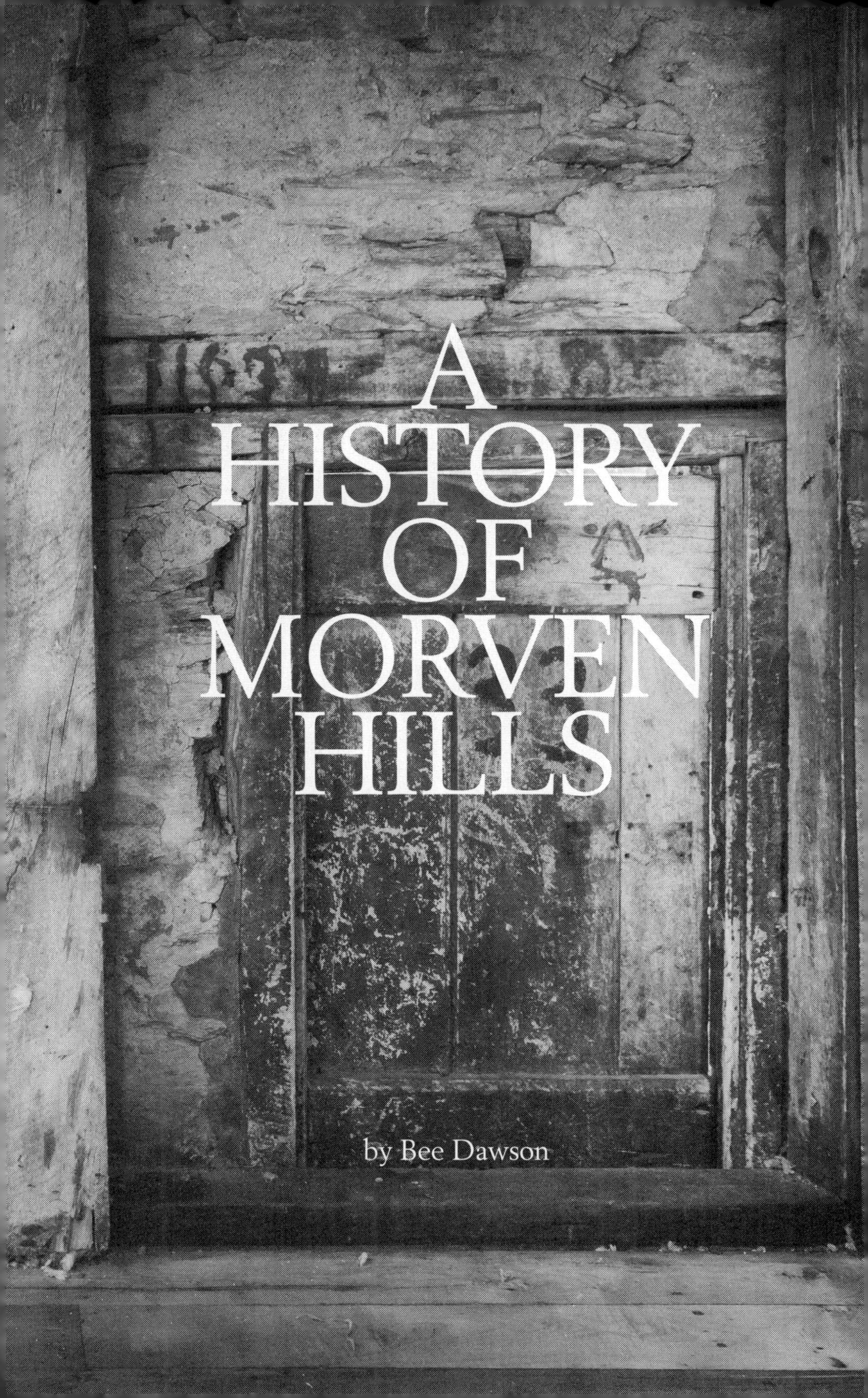

A HISTORY OF MORVEN HILLS

by Bee Dawson

Meet the McLeans

Morven Hills is now a 14,500-hectare tract of land in the Lindis Pass, 30 kilometres from Tarras and 50 kilometres from Omarama. It's just a fraction of its former size; in its heyday it was an enormous sheep station encompassing almost 400,000 acres (162,000 hectares) down the eastern shore of Lake Hawea and the left bank of the Clutha River to Clyde, measuring 75 kilometres from north to south.

WHEN EUROPEANS FIRST ARRIVED in New Zealand they saw vast areas of land that were seemingly free for the taking. The 1855 Waste Lands Act introduced a system of issuing 'depasturing licences' for large areas known as runs or stations. This provided a wonderful opportunity for adventurous souls who were prepared to chance their arm by taking up land in isolated and difficult areas.

Intending settlers would select an area of land and then lodge an application, along with a £20 deposit, with the Commissioner in Dunedin. The application would clearly define where the selected run was, as well as its size and carrying capacity. After the application was approved the runholder had a fixed period in which to stock the run and begin its development. Once these conditions were met they would be granted a 14-year pastoral or grazing licence, in return for an annual licence fee of £5 plus a further £1 for every 1000 sheep above 5000. With such favourable conditions, it is hardly surprising that energetic men with a dollop of capital rushed to the interior.

No land could be distributed before the scope and boundaries of these interior tracts were known. The Otago Provincial Council therefore commissioned John Turnbull Thomson, the recently appointed Chief Surveyor for the Province of Otago, to map the hitherto unexplored areas of the southern South Island. Thomson travelled to Tutuaru, a settlement a few kilometres south of Mataura. Here he consulted with Reko, the Maori chief who had accompanied explorer Nathaniel Chalmers when he ventured into the Upper Clutha area in 1853. Reko told Thomson of the old Maori greenstone trails that went through the inland regions to the West Coast, and also drew a map of the rivers and lakes that would be encountered along the way.

In October 1857 Thomson and a couple of companions set off on horseback at the beginning of his third survey expedition, a reconnaissance through the Upper Waitaki and the area beyond the Dunstan Mountains. Well-laden packhorses would have carried their tools of trade: theodolites, notebooks and pens for recording what they saw, as well as assorted paints, brushes and paper or canvas for the accompanying paintings. There'd have been tents and rolls of blankets, plus a billy, frying pan, large cooking pot and food basics such as oatmeal, flour, salt, tea and sugar. Dogs were useful when it came to catching weka or pukeko (both tasty additions to the stew pot) and ducks were shot whenever the opportunity arose. It was hard work as they needed to cross snow-fed rivers, negotiate steep gorges, and find their way around boulders and through densely growing vegetation such as matagouri and speargrass.

Reko's map must have come into its own once the survey party left Omarama and started to head up the Ahuriri River, a tributary of the Waitaki. In mid-December they reached a low westward-leading pass. Thomson called this 'Lindis' after the Holy Island, Lindisfarne, which lies just off the coast of Northumberland, close to where he'd been born in northeast England. He must have liked the name because, once they'd negotiated the pass, he also named the Lindis River and Lindis Peak.

Thomson now turned away from the river and followed an old Maori track to the summit of one of the local mountains. What he saw from here was unforgettable: 'the Hawea Lake, deep blue, and narrow, surrounded by extensive forests reaching from the snowline to the white gravelly shores: and about five miles westward lay the Wanaka Lake, more open, but broken into promontories and islets and having the peculiarity marked on all Maori sketches, of a long, narrow eastern arm.' Enthralled with the panorama, Thomson named the mountain 'Grandview', sketched the scene and made some notes before the party returned to the Lindis River. Unaware that Chalmers had preceded him by four years, he described his party as 'the first Europeans to sight this interesting district'. It wasn't long before others were equally impressed.

The first Europeans to settle in the Lindis area were the McLeans, Scots who hailed originally from Laghmor on the Isle of Coll, six kilometres west of Mull in Scotland's Inner Hebrides. John McLean (generally known as 'Jock') was well used to challenges. In common with many others, the family had fled poverty and hunger in Scotland. By the middle of the nineteenth century, overpopulation, combined with crop failure and subsequent food shortages, meant that it was almost impossible to live off the land on islands such as Coll. At times conditions were so harsh that islanders survived by eating seaweed and bleeding the cows in order to make black puddings. Many families were also turned off their crofts so as to allow the common land to be enclosed for the exclusive use of the local laird's sheep.

Things were so bad that when Jock's father, Alexander McLean, drowned at sea in 1836, Jock's mother Mary decided that the family should emigrate to a country with better prospects as she could see no future in Scotland for her three sons, Jock (then aged 18), Allan and Robertson, and her two daughters, Mary and Alexandrina. They packed up all their belongings, took a boat to Mull, another to the mainland and eventually found themselves on an emigrant ship bound for Australia.

Once in Australia the three boys found employment as shepherds. No strangers to hard work, they applied themselves with such canny vigour that by 1848 they'd made enough money to buy two sheep stations. When the gold rush began in Victoria in 1851 they set up a gold buying and carrying business — a dangerous occupation, but a lucrative one. In 1852 they heard that land was becoming available in the South Island of New Zealand, so they sold their Australian interests and set sail across the Tasman.

Shortly after arriving in New Zealand the McLeans purchased Ashfield, a 10,000-acre (4047-hectare) property near Christchurch. In 1855 they also bought a 30,000-acre (12,141-hectare) farm close to Ashburton which they named Laghmor after their home in Coll. This would have been enough for most people but the energetic McLeans thrived on challenges.

When, in 1858, a passing Maori told the then 40-year-old Jock of a great inland tract of land that had not yet been settled by Europeans, the thought was irresistible. Leaving his brothers in charge, Jock rode off to the Waitaki River, engaged the Maori chief Huruhuru as a guide and set off to explore inland Otago. After crossing the Waitaki on a raft made of korari (flax), the intrepid pair headed up the south bank as far as Omarama, pressed on up the Ahuriri River and then continued over the Lindis Pass. When Jock climbed Mt Grandview and saw the great expanse of potential sheep country that stretched over to lakes Hawea and Wanaka, he determined to make it his own.

The Waste Land Board had divided this vast tract of land into four units with the intention that no single applicant would be granted more than one property. The answer was to make it a family affair — Jock and three of his siblings each applied for a run, with the idea that they would later amalgamate the land and run it as one station. It worked a treat. On 3 September 1858, Jock was granted the licence for Run 235 (33,184 hectares); sister Alexandrina was allotted the licence for Run 236 (48,562 hectares); and brothers Allan and Robertson were allotted Runs 237 (26,709 hectares) and 238 (33,994 hectares) respectively. It seems strange that the Waste Land Board doesn't appear to have suspected anything odd about all four applicants sharing a surname and place of residence.

Jock and Allan took over the development and management of this huge pastoral empire — a pear-shaped area of over 160,000 hectares covered with luxuriant grass and native vegetation — and called it 'Morven Hills'. There's a legend that Jock McLean named the property after a Scottish ancestor, the Baronet of Morven, but in fact there has never been a baronetcy of Morven. It's likely that McLean named the station after the hills of his beloved Scotland, and that Morven Hills is a spelling corruption of the Scottish Morvern Hills, quite close to Oban. They have an unmistakable similarity.

There was no opportunity for the McLean family to sit back and quietly contemplate their new purchase as, under the terms of the licence, the run had to be stocked within a certain time. The brothers would have soon realised that this was an impossible task — even if there had been enough sheep available in Otago, it would have taken months to stock the station. It was necessary to be a little canny. The story goes that when the inspector from the Lands Department arrived at Morven Hills to check on sheep numbers, Jock received him with true Highland hospitality — plentiful food washed down with generous amounts of Scotland's best malt. The next morning probably started a little slowly, but there was still plenty of time for Jock to take the inspector to a vantage point from which he could see thousands of grazing sheep. Satisfied with the day's work, the two adjourned to Jock's hut where they quaffed many more drams. What the inspector didn't realise was that while they were drinking and swapping yarns, Jock's shepherds were quietly mustering the sheep and moving them to another block. When that block was viewed the next day the officer was impressed with how well it was stocked. This rigmarole continued for an undefined number of days until, after several bottles of whisky and much nocturnal shifting of sheep, the officer returned to Dunedin entirely satisfied that the requirements of the Land Office had been met.

It's impossible to know if this story is true, but in 1860 William Logie, the Chief Inspector of Sheep for North Otago, noted that the McLean brothers owned 18,000 sheep out of a total of 137,000 in the Southern District. By 1863 Morven Hills was recorded as having 40,000 sheep and in 1868, 82,000. By 1871 the numbers had grown to 110,000 and when the property was sold in 1874, 140,000 sheep. This is probably as many as the run ever carried. From this point the rapid increase of the rabbit population, and the associated degradation of pastures, meant that the carrying capacity of all runs in Otago plummeted.

In 1866 the McLeans added to their already huge estates by taking up Waikakahi Station north of the Waitaki River, and while 'Big Jock' continued to attend to the running of Morven Hills, his brother Allan began to spend more and more of his time at the new property. When Waikakahi Station was subdivided in 1898, part of it was used for the township of Morven. Once the property was sold Allan moved to Christchurch and built 'Holly Lea', the largest wooden house in New Zealand, later known as 'McLean's Mansion'.

MANY OF THE SHEPHERDS on Morven Hills were also of Scottish origin. Used to the rigours of the Highlands, these self-sufficient and frugal men adapted well to the isolated station life. Indeed, anyone wandering unawares into a gathering of these men in the Ardgour district at the south end of Morven Hills might have been excused for thinking himself back in Scotland, as many of the men had only a few words of English and conversed solely in Gaelic.

Workers were always a mixed bag, ranging from dour Scottish shepherds to the occasional well-connected remittance man. Although many loved the isolated life, some found it came at a cost. The *Otago Daily Times* of 15 June 1883 reported the sad case of Morven Hills shepherd John Oswald Stewart who cut his throat with a pocketknife after a drinking binge. Two of his fellow shepherds put him in a buggy and took him to the Cromwell District Hospital, but he died shortly after they arrived. Originally from Glasgow, Stewart had spent almost five years at Morven Hills. After noting that he was single and had no relations in the colony, the newspaper went on to record that he was a well-educated man, who 'was in receipt of regular remittances from Home, which unhappily induced him at times to that over-indulgence which ultimately led to his tragical fate.'

Shearing was always the busiest period on the run. In the week or so before it started, shepherds would muster great flocks of sheep off the surrounding hills. The first job was to wash them to remove the worst of the dirt and grease that compromised the quality of the fleeces. After the sheep had been put through a stone dip at the aptly named 'Dip Creek' they'd have been turned out on Camp Hill until their wool was dry. Then they were mustered for a second time and taken to the shearing shed.

When shearing was about to start, scores of shearers converged on the station headquarters in search of work.

Tough men all, they'd have thought nothing of walking for many kilometres across hard country and often did so in challenging weather. On one occasion John McKenzie, a shearer known as the 'Highland Chief', 'cut out' at Omarama Station at 5.30 p.m., shouldered his swag and then walked all night in order to be ready to start at Morven Hills at 5.30 the next morning.

There was no knowing how many shearers and shed-hands would turn up — in the early morning those that had arrived in the middle of the night could be found scattered around the buildings, sleeping wherever they could find a sheltered spot. Once sufficient numbers of shearers and hands had been engaged, those who had missed out were given a ticket which entitled them to a free meal at the cookhouse and then sent packing. This scene would be repeated at the Ardgour outstation as well as other stations in the area.

Shearers had to be hardy to cope with primitive conditions, long hours and low wages. In 1867 when manager John McLean (no relation to Jock McLean, who owned the land) advertised for 20 shearers, he noted that they'd be paid 17/6 for every hundred sheep shorn, in addition to their keep. However, by 1870 the price had dropped to 15 shillings per hundred, plus rations. The cook was also paid on output — 4½d for every meal supplied.

Once the shearing was done, bullock wagons would be loaded with the wool — there were usually up to 30 bales on each, but when there was a larger wagon and bigger team, more could be carried. Generally there were three teams, each consisting of 14 bullocks. The trip began with a long hard grind over the first 10 or 12 kilometres from the woolshed to the pass, but the going was much easier once they were heading downhill. It could take up to three weeks to travel from the station down the Waitaki to Oamaru.

Two or more wagons would travel together so that they could help each other when they came to river crossings and swamps. If a load got bogged, as many as 30 bullocks would be yoked together while their drivers cracked their whips and urged on the struggling beasts, swearing loudly all the time.

top
A load of wool from Morven Hills is carried over the pass by bullock teams, 1894.

bottom
Some of the Morven Hills Station workers in the early 1870s, including the owner John (Jock) McLean (centre rear) and servant Fan So (right), who worked for the McLean family for 33 years.

The colourful language was seldom censored for an audience. It is said that when a somewhat shocked squatter's wife chided one driver, saying, 'Oh John, where did you learn to swear so?' he replied coldly, 'You couldn't learn it, ma'am, it's a gift.'

During these early station years properties were still largely unfenced, meaning that a careful eye had to be kept on the whereabouts of stock. The shepherds and boundary keepers who lived in small huts in far-flung corners of the station were charged with preventing sheep from straying onto neighbouring runs. Theirs was a very hard and lonely life — from time to time one of these men would walk or ride to meet the keeper on the next beat, but other than that they would seldom see anyone. Few of the men were married — these outposts of settlement were generally considered to be too lonely and too tough for family life.

Although the vast expanses of tussock land initially looked ideal for sheep, settlers soon discovered that the tall tussocks, coarse grass and fern weren't particularly palatable. The solution was to burn the established vegetation in order to encourage new shoots. Fortunately Jock and Allan were relatively restrained when it came to burning their tussock land. Whereas some settlers would set light to tussock whenever it took their fancy, the McLeans realised that it was important to give the pastures ample time to recover, so restricted their burning to springtime. There was still damage done, however, as the regenerated tussock grassland was different from what was there before. Tall tussocks gave way to shorter varieties and fine native grasses were replaced by the less palatable silver tussock, speargrass, Maori onion and kanuka. Introduced plants also became common, as clover and grass seeds were often scattered over the ashes. The burning, combined with over-stocking, meant that pastures quickly became degraded.

THERE WAS ALWAYS a warm welcome at Morven Hills homestead. The memory of the extreme poverty of his childhood in Scotland never left Jock. Determined that no one should starve on his land, he was known to declare, 'If there was only one merino left on Morven Hills, I'd share it with a swagger.' Although there was never any danger of the station being down to its last sheep, there were plenty of swaggers who benefited from the station's hospitality.

There were many other visitors as well. Guests included family and friends, other aspiring run-holders, a smattering of sheep inspectors and, in March 1867, the Governor of New Zealand, Sir George Grey. When at Morven Hills the Governor took such a fancy to a couple of the sheepdogs that Jock gave them to Grey as a present.

Although a bachelor establishment, the homestead was ably run by a series of housekeepers, generally wives of shepherds who were working on the station. In the late 1860s, shepherd John Polson and his wife Christina moved into the homestead so that Christina could keep house for Jock McLean. The next 10 years kept her very busy as, in addition to her paid duties, she bore six children.

The most valued servant was possibly Fan So, a Chinese man who had first earned the gratitude of the McLean family in Australia. The McLeans were working as carriers on the Victoria diggings when Fan So heard of a plot to attack them and steal a consignment of gold. Greatly concerned for their safety, he swam a river in order to warn the brothers of their danger. As a result of this he was given a permanent place in the McLean household. In all, Fan So worked for the family for 33 years.

Jock was known as a kind and generous employer, and was greatly respected by the many people who worked on the station. When he finally left Morven Hills he was presented with a £20 gold watch as a mark of the station workers' esteem.

Jock was appointed to the Legislative Council in 1871 and was a member until its abolition in 1875. From the time of his appointment he spent increasingly long periods in Wellington, leaving most of the affairs of the station in the hands of his manager. At about this time he bought two properties in North Otago and built a large house at Redcastle near Oamaru. After Jock's death in 1902, his specific wish was to be buried in the Addington Cemetery alongside his mother and elder sister Mary, who had both predeceased him, in 1871 and 1875 respectively.

top
A wagonload of wool leaves
Morven Hills, 1900.

bottom
The original stables at
Morven Hills.

Shearing in the early days

Once the McLeans had taken up the land, the next thing to think about was accommodation.

THE SITE JOCK SELECTED for the station headquarters was about 13 kilometres from the summit of the Lindis Pass. At this point the Lindis Valley opened out so there was a reasonable amount of flat land with good sun for much of the day. Temporary living quarters were thrown up. Although these corrugated-iron huts lacked any sort of insulation, they provided valuable shelter while the McLeans and their men got established.

Superb building material was right at hand. After the schist rocks and rubble that lay around the building site had been gathered, more would have been quarried from the hill behind. Once they had been sorted and shaped, stonemasons used them to build the homestead, a solid stone building in the style of the crofters' cottages of the Scottish Highlands. Although it is possible that the homestead was initially thatched with the abundant long grass that grew close by, it is more likely that the galvanised-iron roof was there from the beginning. In later years more rooms were added but these were constructed of adobe bricks made from local clay and fired on site. The stonemason must have forgotten that he'd crossed the equator, as he set the house facing southeast. He built a long verandah facing the river, but it's on the cold side of the house, so never sees the sun.

Cold or not, the homestead soon developed a certain rustic charm. In Richard Norman's 'rural rambles', published in the *Otago Witness* of 28 April 1892, he recalled how the Lindis Valley

> opens out a mile or two in width, in the centre of which is the original station homestead. This place strongly reminds us of pictures of English rural life . . . An acre or two of the large oxeye or buckeye daisy when in full bloom and vigour as it is to be seen here is a most beautiful sight. The large-leaved dock is here grown in great profusion . . . There are also quantities of yarrow grass and some other kinds, all growing in the most magnificent profusion.
>
> Then the homestead is nearly surrounded by willow and poplar trees, some of them of large size and many upwards of 30 years old. Mr John Carter, the first manager of the Wanaka station, brought the first willow and poplar cuttings on horseback from Christchurch, and as these trees grew up cuttings were sent to all the neighbouring places.

Four woolsheds are known to have been built during the early years of the original Morven Hills run. The first was built at Breast Hill, some 10 kilometres from the homestead. The site for this would have been selected with the view that the closer

The original homestead at Morven Hills.

the shed was to the boundary, the closer the wool was to the market. In the early days of settlement it was always easier to let the wool move on the hoof. However, as roads became better and communications easier, this woolshed's isolation lost its appeal and in 1890 manager John Stronach called for tenders for its dismantling and re-erection.

Once the southern portions of the run were stocked, an outstation was built quite close to the old Ardgour Station. This included a sizeable iron woolshed with stands for 28 shearers, as well as a wool scouring plant and press, men's quarters, a cookshop and a homestead. A third (wooden) woolshed was built at Tarras after the Ardgour shed burned down in the 1880s.

But the most famous woolshed of all is the huge stone building that dominates the Lindis Valley at Morven Hills. This magnificent building is T-shaped and had two shearing boards, with a total of 34 stands for blade shearers. The shearing area and the adjacent catching pens are well lit from dormer windows, with a series of small windows above the portholes. The wool room extends across the top end of the shed and was spacious enough to hold the very large wool clips of that era until they were carted over the Lindis by bullock teams.

Black beech is the dominant timber. The timber mill was situated at Makarora, at the head of Lake Wanaka, and by 1861 they were floating beech logs down the lake. The original roof, still unpainted, was made from Scottish corrugated iron and has survived a century of storms and blizzards. In those days there was a significant class distinction, with two doors adjacent to each other, one for the boss and one for the workers, both leading to the same area. Rumour has it, that if a worker went through the boss's door, he was fired.

The woolshed's date of origin is something of a mystery. Madge's theory is that it was built between 1861 and 1863. At that time, the hundreds of gold diggers who were camped in the valley were becoming discontented as they discovered how little gold there was. McLean, astute man that he was, may have decided to use the manpower that suddenly materialised on his doorstep, fed them and then put them to work building the great shed. The cookshop was also built around about this time and it's not hard to imagine the camaraderie that existed among hundreds of happy miners, with food in their bellies, and cash in their hands.

Of course, the theory about the woolshed being built around 1861 may be wrong. Many people have looked into this but none have found evidence to support any definite date. Geoffrey Thornton, author of *The New Zealand Heritage of Farm Buildings*, and Heritage New Zealand both opt for 1873. Others suggest 1880 as the date of origin.

There is no sound evidence of a woolshed being near the Morven Hills homestead prior to the 1890s. Contemporary accounts generally indicate that the only woolshed in the vicinity was the one at Breast Hill. When the Reverend Todd, of St Paul's Presbyterian Church, Oamaru, made a mission tour through the county of Waitaki in 1879, he wrote that after leaving the top of the Lindis Pass at three in the afternoon, his party reached the woolshed at four. Once arrived they found a busy scene: '. . . a number of men were scouring wool, and among them two or three Maoris who had come from the encampment. I held a short service at the shepherd's house at the woolshed and arranged to hold another on Monday evening on my way back.' There is no doubt that he is referring to the woolshed at Breast Hill, as he later refers to it as being six miles above the station.

After this the Reverend pressed on down the valley, crossing the Lindis River six times before he reached Morven Hills, 'situated in the Lindis Valley, overshadowed by high mountains'. The Reverend noted: 'After tea held a meeting with the shepherds in the house, my subject being the two debtors as contained in Luke vii., 36–50.' On the next day, the Sabbath, 23 March, he had two more meetings and also visited the men in their houses. Although a great recorder of detail, the good Reverend makes no mention of any woolshed at this site. This is hardly surprising, as it is unlikely that two woolsheds would have been operating in such close proximity to each other.

There's no doubt that the Breast Hill woolshed was still standing the next year as, in August 1890, tenders were sought for dismantling and re-erecting the 'Upper Morven Hills woolshed'. No one disputes that it was dismantled, but there is confusion as to whether or not it was ever rebuilt. When Madge interviewed Mrs Carlsen, a former housekeeper at Malvern Downs, she was told the Breast Hill woolshed had been dismantled and re-erected 'at the homestead'. Madge always believed that this homestead was the house that manager John Stronach had built on a knoll at Tarras in 1885, which he called The Homestead, and that this is where the Breast Hill woolshed was shifted to — not the old house at Morven Hills.

Richard Norman may have settled the matter in his 'rural rambles' article of 28 April 1892. When describing his stay at Morven Hills, Norman was very admiring of the station woolshed which '. . . used to be about six miles further on, but this year Mr John Stronach, the manager, had it moved to this centre so as to be nearer Tarras, which is now the homestead. It is built of stone and roofed with iron, and the yards are erected on a new plan, the whole of the work reflecting great credit on the contractors, Messrs Gair and Leslie, with whom I stopped the night.'

Norman appears to have had no doubt that the woolshed had just been moved to its new site over the river from the Morven Hills homestead. As we don't know how big the original woolshed at Breast Hill was, it may be that significant extensions were made once it was re-erected. But even this is dubious as, although the writer mentions the new plan for the yards, he doesn't say a word about changes to the woolshed. One presumes that Norman stayed with the contractors because they were still on site while finishing the job.

When a 'Canterbury Girl' wrote in the *Press* in 1914 of visiting Morven Hills, she was impressed by the woolshed:

> Early the next morning we went over the woolshed, which is built on the most up-to-date lines. We were pleasantly surprised at the state of

cleanliness and order that reigned. One thinks of a woolshed at shearing time as a place to get out of as speedily as possible but that was not the case at Morven Hills. Although just after six, the ten machines, worked by benzoline, were all clipping busily. The shearer has long hours, and works from six in the morning till six at night. A good man accounts for 200 sheep a day, and as £1 is paid for each hundred, a shearer ought soon to possess sheep of his own. Their calling certainly produces finely developed specimens of manhood; a Sandow [a pioneering bodybuilder] might well be proud of their muscular arm development.

> We were surprised at the great variety in the texture of the wool and the care necessary in the grading. The fleeces varied in colour, too, from an occasional black and brown to a bright yellow. Jason coming to this woolshed in search of a golden fleece need have gone no further. We left the woolshed feeling quite the wool experts, and with our sheep knowledge considerably increased.

The large number of stands would certainly have been necessary in the pre-rabbit heyday of the station. In 1868 Jock McLean estimated the worth of the previous season's clip as being over £35,000, and when the McLeans sold Morven Hills in 1874, sheep numbers totalled more than 140,000. Elsewhere it is recorded that Morven Hills once shore 150,000 sheep and tailed 10,000 lambs in one season. However, by 1890 this number would have declined significantly as rabbits were competing for any pasture that they didn't destroy. This fact alone makes it unlikely that the woolshed would have been extended at any time after the 1880s.

On 12 January 1900 the *Marlborough Express* reported that on the last day of the Morven Hills shearing, 30 shearers put up a record. The total average of sheep shorn was 141 per man, the ringer shearing 198.

In 1908 it was reported that the greatest number of sheep

ever shorn in one day at Morven Hills was 4812 — almost 145 per stand. This average was brought up by the very best shearers who would shear over 190 a day, with the exceptional few managing over 200.

IN THE EARLY YEARS of the station, the sheep would be washed before they were shorn in order to get rid of the large amounts of dirt and other matter that clogged up the wool. This could account for up to 26 per cent of the weight of the fleece. However, by the 1870s this system had given way to one in which the wool was scoured after the sheep were shorn. The scouring vats were filled with water, which was heated with the help of iron boilers. The next step was to add soap. It was important to choose carefully, as a very alkaline soap would remove too much grease, meaning that the wool would lose its pliancy and soft springiness. Once the fleeces had been put into the sudsy solution, men would stir the fleeces with large sticks until all the wool was thoroughly scoured. The fleeces were then drained, rinsed thoroughly to remove all the loose dirt and scouring solution, drained again and then taken by hand-carts to be spread out in the sun to dry before they were collected up again for baling.

After the wooden woolshed was built at Tarras in the 1880s, shorn fleeces were baled and then carted by bullock wagon to the old woolshed at Morven Hills, where the wool was scoured before it was dried, baled again and sent to market by bullock cart.

Prior to shearing, gangs of musterers brought in huge flocks of several thousand sheep to the holding paddocks at the shearing sheds. Here they were handed over to shepherds who carried out all the subsequent yarding, drafting and branding operations.

At this time the shearing was done mainly by gangs of Australian shearers, who received 15/- per hundred sheep.

This was somewhat less than 30 years before, when 17/6 was the standard rate. Food was pretty basic as well. John McArthur, a shearer at Morven Hills in 1890, later recalled:

> The menu in those days consisted of mutton, bread, sugar, tea, salt and potatoes. The cook was generally a baker and made the bread. He used to take a 'cut' off the dough in the trough and add some mutton fat and brown sugar. This, when baked in the oven, was called 'brownie' and wasn't bad when properly made. We got no butter and no spices and of course no jam.
>
> The hut and the sheds were usually built alongside a running creek or river. That was our wash-basin and where we washed our clothes. I will now describe our sleeping accommodation. I saw one hut measured with the rule. It was twenty-one feet by twelve. There were eighteen men sleeping in that hut. There were three tiers of bunks right round, built in six by two for a man, usually no mattresses — at least the station didn't provide any. If there happened to be a straw stack handy some of us would use straw, but as a rule all we had on the bare boards was an empty wool bale.

Shearing continued for weeks over summer, the Christmas season included. However, there was always some light relief on Christmas Day. From about 1870 to at least 1885 the Morven Hills sports were an annual Christmas event. Organised by the shearers and shed-hands, the 17 different events included activities as diverse as throwing the hammer; running high jump; hop, step and jump; wrestling; sack races; and the three-legged race. In 1884 the 300-yards race fielded an impressive 40 competitors, whereas the 'old men's race' attracted just nine contestants. The most strenuous event was inevitably the 'shearers and shed-hands versus all-comers tug-of-war', but the greatest hilarity was reserved for the 'wheeling barrow blindfolded' event.

The Dalgety era and beyond

Early in 1874 the McLeans sold Morven Hills to Colonel George Whitmore, of Rissington in Hawke's Bay, for a massive £128,000. Included in the price was the station's stock: 140,000 sheep, 40 working bullocks, 200 cattle and 50 horses. After the sale, Jock McLean took himself off to Redcastle in Oamaru and concentrated on his political career.

A VETERAN OF THE LAND WARS and a regular officer in the Imperial Army, Colonel Whitmore had already established himself as a land-owner in Hawke's Bay. And that is where he decided to stay. It's not known whether he suddenly got cold feet after buying Morven Hills or just relished the chance to make a quick profit. Whatever the reason, he'd owned the station for less than a month when he resold it to James Cogle of Lauder Station for £2000 more than he'd paid for it. Like Whitmore, Cogle appears to have been more interested in making a quick buck than actually farming the land, and by November 1874 he was negotiating the sale of the station to F.G. Dalgety and his associate, Charles Nichols.

A letter from Cogle at the time of the sale reads:

> *Nov 12, 1874:* My Dear Nichols, Your telegram of yesterday's date re Dalgety's message, to hand today. The offer can remain open till the 15th Dec if you wish it. It might be a little awkward in case a Melbourne buyer came over — but I have no doubt I could get him to wait. I have fully made up my mind not to offer it to anyone else at the figure named. It would pay me better to keep it for another year. Considering the high price of wool and the tremendous rise in the price of cattle since the offer was made, I think I have offered it below its value. But of course I would rather sell to a man like Dalgety (where I know everything would be perfectly safe) than I would for a few thousand more to a risky party.
> I remain, J. Cogle.

A London-born Scot, Frederick Gonnerman Dalgety was just 16 years old when he arrived in Sydney in 1834. By the time he was 24 he'd already gained enough experience in the business world to become manager of a new wool-trading firm in Melbourne, and in 1846 set up his own firm, Dalgety & Company. The firm focused on supplying the needs of those who had settled on the land, providing squatters with goods and buying their produce. During the gold rushes of the 1850s Dalgety extended his service to the gold diggers and made a considerable amount of money from speculating in gold.

So well did he prosper, that within the space of six years Dalgety was able to move back to England, set up a branch of the business in London and acquire a country estate in

Hampshire. Dalgety also set up branches in New Zealand. The first two, Dalgety & Buckley (in Lyttelton) and Dalgety & Rattray (Dunedin) were followed by further branches around New Zealand. Dalgety also began to invest in New Zealand land. In 1866 he acquired an interest in Omarama Station, followed by Hawkdun (1867), Balmoral (1872), Morven Hills (1878), Ruakitura (1884) and Grasmere (1892).

When Dalgety visited New Zealand for the first and only time in 1881, he spent three months touring the country and inspecting his properties. After the business was converted to a limited liability company in 1884 the name was changed to Dalgety & Co. At this point Dalgety became the chairman of directors. He died in 1894, aged 76.

Although Dalgety often tried to involve his family in the firm, he was consistently disappointed. Brought up in English gentry comfort, his sons chose easy country lives over the cut and thrust of the business world. It is said that when one son, Charles, lost interest after a brief foray into business, Dalgety was so disgusted that he sent him out to New Zealand.

Dalgety's Dunedin manager, who had been instructed to teach the errant lad something about sheep, dispatched Charles to Omarama Station. Charles probably wasn't any more interested in sheep than in the business side of the firm, but at least he found love. He hadn't been at Omarama for long before he met and married the daughter of W. Burnett, manager of Hawkdun Station. Burnett, who in addition to managing Hawkdun was responsible for keeping an eye on Morven Hills and Omarama, is sure to have been delighted at a match with one of Dalgety's sons.

FROM 1874 TO 1910 Morven Hills was run by a succession of managers who were appointed by, and responsible to, the manager of Dalgety's Dunedin branch. The first of the managers, J. McLean (no relation of the former owners), had been a shepherd on the station for many years before taking on the management role. He was followed by Alex McPhail, who was assisted by John Dewar as manager at the Ardgour end of the station.

John Stronach, the manager from 1883 to 1894, oversaw a challenging decade. For a start he had to deal with the Long Depression of the 1880s when prices for wool fell, rabbits invaded the station and the land started to show signs of serious erosion. During this time massive unemployment meant that there were many men on the roads — in 1892 Morven Hills station reported that 400 tramps had sought jobs during the past year.

Stronach had hardly had time to settle in before the Ardgour woolshed, scouring plant and press were all destroyed by fire. Rather than reconstruct everything as it had been, Stronach reorganised the station so that the headquarters were at Tarras, as this was closer both to the busy new commercial centre of Cromwell and to the road that went through the Cromwell Gorge to Dunedin. At Tarras, he built a new homestead, a large wooden woolshed, shearers' quarters, a cookhouse and other necessary buildings. Once he and his family had moved into the homestead, the old headquarters in the Lindis Valley became an outstation.

In 1890 Stronach further decided that the woolshed at Breast Hill was inconveniently remote, so he had it dismantled and re-erected. Although there is some dispute as to where its final resting place was, some consider that the new location was over the river from the homestead at the Morven Hills outstation in the Lindis Valley. Six miles closer to Tarras than Breast Hill, this was a much more centralised location for the shed.

During his time Stronach planted hundreds of trees around the homestead at Tarras. He also entered local-body politics and represented Lindis on the Vincent County Council for two terms.

Thomas McWhirter, the manager from 1894 to 1905, was concerned about the wrangling that took place between shearers and their employers before shearing started every year. His leadership abilities were ably demonstrated in 1895,

'The Homestead' at Tarras, built by John Stronach,
was the second house built on Morven Hills.

when the *Oamaru Mail* of 18 February reported that the manager at Morven Hills was

> a man who evidently thoroughly understands both sides of the question, and who by his example proves that he is a gentleman who can lead his fellow men. Instead of the usual yearly agreement three quarters of a yard long between manager and men, the former stepped into the shed with 'Now men, my agreement for you is this: you shear and I pay.' The result of this short arrangement was that everyone did his very best, the shearing was got through in a much shorter time than has been for years on Morven Hills, and the wool was a larger clip. At the finish of shearing one of the leaders came forward and in the name of the others thanked Mr McWhirter for his kind manner towards them, and the men then gave him three cheers that might have been heard at Cromwell. Responding, the manager thanked them for their services, and wished they might all be spared to come back. That's one example of how a large shearing can be got through without disagreements or squabble of any sort.

McWhirter found black sheep to be a profitable sideline and by 1899 had a flock that numbered nearly 1000. The *Ellesmere Guardian* of 25 February reported: 'He finds that black wool commands from 1d to 2d a pound more than white. It is used to make the garments of an order of monks, whose rules oblige them to wear clothes made of undyed black wool. The experiment and its result will be watched with interest by those concerned in sheep-breeding.' By the time McWhirter retired the flock was 5000 strong.

R.K. Smith took over the running of the station in 1906 and placed a greater emphasis on raising the standard of the flock.

IN 1906 ROBERT KERMODE SMITH (always referred to as R.K.) took over the reins at Morven Hills, supported by his brother-in-law William Ross Mackay, who had married R.K.'s sister Margaret Ethel. R.K. placed great emphasis on improving the standard of the Morven Hills flock, so he must have been very pleased when, less than a year after he took over the station management, the *Mataura Ensign* of 26 February 1907 reported that the Morven Hills Station clip had been an exceptionally good one, with the average fleece weight of the 48,000 sheep shorn at the first shearing being 9¼ pounds (4.2 kilograms). 'The sheep are in splendid order, and this must be a record for merino sheep from any large station in Otago.'

Later that year R.K. imported Australian merinos from the celebrated Uardray flock in New South Wales in order to improve his flocks. Numbers rose steadily and in 1909 Morven Hills shore 63,000 sheep.

Charlie Norman, who had mustered on Morven Hills in 1909, returned in March 1982, a fine old gentleman aged 89 and with a mind as sharp as a pin. He was obviously wrapped in nostalgia and wanted to see the shed again. In his day, in 1909, they shore 63,000 sheep. The wage in those days was £1 a week and Charlie reiterated what was already known — R.K. treated his men well, but if anyone wrote or carved their name in the shed, they were down the road. Madge also remembers a loader driver telling her about his uncle Morven Campbell who had been born on Morven Hills in 1894 when his father was a shepherd.

When Morven Hills was subdivided in 1910 R.K. moved to Tarras where he bought 'Beauly Farm' from John McRae, renaming it Malvern Downs. Never one to do things by halves, he set to and planted 5000 pine trees on his Tarras property. In 1913 he purchased Tarras Station from George Collins. In May 1924 R.K. sold Malvern Downs Station to Hector Gibson (Madge's father), held a clearing sale and left on a visit to South Africa and Rhodesia. Sadly his retirement was short-lived — R.K. died shortly after his return in 1925.

BY 1882 THE PRESSURE to make more land available for settlement was so intense that the Land Board put out a subdivision of Central Otago run Mt Pisa and then began to subdivide other runs. Dalgety and Nichols' Morven Hills was cut into 23 blocks. However, the great jubilation and optimism amongst the many intending farmers who wanted to buy land quickly turned to bitter disappointment when the existing lessees bought back all the land. No one else stood a chance.

The agitation for closer land settlement continued to rumble away. There was huge resentment of the 'great sheep lords' who had been allowed to lease massive areas of land, and were able to make large amounts of money while no one else had a chance to own their own farm. In the middle of 1904 things came to a head once again, with the circulation of land petitions that called on the government to subdivide runs. By August 1907 it had been decided that the Morven Hills run would again be subdivided in early 1910. It was pointed out that once this was done, initial rentals should be moderate as the rabbits had done so much damage that 'the new settlers will have to redeem a desert'.

When the massive 363,976-acre (147,296-hectare) Morven Hills run was split up in a public ballot in February 1910, each applicant was examined in order to assess whether he was suitable as a prospective run-holder. The subdivision of the station was accompanied by another huge task — the mustering and selling of all the stock on the station. Weeks were spent mustering sheep from all corners of the property and bringing them to Tarras, the headquarters of Morven Hills. Five kilometres of wire netting were used to construct special yards 400 metres long.

Dalgety & Co looked after intending buyers very well. Transport was provided from Cromwell and accommodation provided at Tarras for anyone who had to stay overnight. During the day, lunch and afternoon tea were laid out in a

top
The Lindis Hotel, 1902.

bottom
Lindis Pass School, 1936.

great marquee, with large numbers of waiters in attendance.

The *Otago Daily Times* of 31 March 1910 reported that 'the bulk of the sheep were strong and healthy, and in good condition, notwithstanding the fact that they had been in hand for a fortnight, and to a certain extent had lost their bloom.' The only exception was the lambs, which, owing to the very dry weather experienced in that part of the country, and the consequent scarcity of feed, were not so well-grown or in such good condition as they might have been. A large number of the merinos were purchased by buyers who had secured runs at the sale and ballot of Morven Hills, while large mobs were driven to South Canterbury and Southland.

'In all 49,849 merinos, 18,254 half bred sheep and 299 merino rams were offered for sale, a total of over 68,000 sheep. Auctioneering was so brisk that this enormous number of sheep was disposed of in less than three hours.'

Once the stock had gone many other items were sold off — the complete clearance sale took almost a week.

Rabbits, rabbits and more rabbits

WANTED, at once, for Morven Hills Station,
Twenty Good RABBITERS.
Apply John Stronach, Manager Morven Hills.

— OAMARU MAIL, 6 JUNE 1890

The settlers who released the first rabbits somewhere near Invercargill in early 1864 did so with the best of intentions.

LIKE THE DEER, the rabbits would provide sport for the gentry, but would also provide food for all country folk in the tradition of Mother England. Never in their wildest dreams could these settlers have foreseen the disastrous effect the rabbits would have on the countryside.

Unchecked by predators, the new immigrants ate, bred prolifically, ate more, bred more and suddenly were out of control. Uneasiness at the speed of their spread was starting to stir by 1876, just 12 years after the first rabbits were released. By the time another five years had passed, things were looking grim. The rabbits gobbled the grass intended for sheep, eating the leaves so closely to the ground that whole areas of grassland were ruined. Hundreds of thousands of sheep starved and died. Many high-country runs were so affected that large areas were either partially or fully abandoned, and sheep numbers plummeted to the extent that many land-holders faced ruin. The situation was so bad that in March 1881 the first rabbit control districts were defined. By 1885 extensive portions of the larger runs were being offered at reduced rentals in the hope that someone would have sufficient courage to take them up. At Morven Hills the 6640-acre (2687-hectare) Run 236d was offered for 10 years at a rent of £100.

A small army of men was employed to combat the pest at Morven Hills. Armed with an arsenal of guns, traps and pickaxes, as well as dogs and ferrets, these men were sent out into the hills, tasked with killing as many rabbits as possible. The offensive was so well organised that the humourists of the *Cromwell Argus* suggested that on one station the hands used javelins and boomerangs, and that on another a stock whip was being used to mow down the rows as the rabbit hordes approached!

Irrespective of the methods used, rabbiting was a hard and lonely occupation. Properties were divided into rabbiting blocks, each of which was allotted to an experienced rabbiter. A hack to ride and a good retriever dog, a supply of spring traps, an adze and a good sharp pocketknife were the essential items of the rabbiter's equipment, along with poison baits. Pelts were at their best over winter so rabbiters would work from late autumn to early spring and then find alternative employment as musterers, shearers, shed-hands or casual farm-workers during the summer. Living was tough — rabbiters would sleep in huts if they were lucky, but otherwise had to tough it out in tents. The fires that they used for warmth and cooking were fuelled by the twigs and branches of the thorny matagouri. As for food, there was generally a steady diet of rabbit (great in stew), supplemented by mutton, bread and oatmeal with a touch of plum jam for flavouring.

It was a hard life, but it could be a lucrative one. When skins were fetching 2/6d each a good living could be made by a skilled rabbiter. Irrespective of how many rabbits were killed, however, there always seemed to be enough left for reinfestation. There were some cynical souls who asked, how many of those who made a living from rabbiting were interested in total extermination?

During the first half of 1884, 102,000 rabbits were taken off Morven Hills. This must have helped for a while, but numbers soon bounced back. In 1892 it was recorded that half a million rabbits had been destroyed on the Tarras and Morven Hills runs. Removing the rabbits, or even reducing them to manageable numbers, seemed an impossible task. By the late 1890s the Morven Hills flock had plummeted from a peak of about 134,000 (when the McLeans sold the property in 1874) to just 70,000 sheep.

Matters improved from 1897 onwards, when Thomas McWhirter, manager at Morven Hills, switched from using poisoned oats to poisoned pollard (wheat bran). This was so successful that it quickly became the preferred method and probably marked the turn of the tide. Although rabbits continued to be a significant problem, they were never again as bad as during the three decades prior to 1900.

In January 1910, just prior to the subdivision of the station, it was estimated that the cost of coping with the rabbit pest on Morven Hills had averaged about £4000 over the previous five years. The *Mataura Ensign* of 25 June 1910 reported that 20,000 rabbits had been taken off one of the new Morven Hills blocks since the land was taken up in April — a period of less than 10 weeks' working time. 'At the present price of skins these should average about £2 each so that the two men should have close on £200 each for their labour.'

During the first few decades of the twentieth century, freelance rabbiters appeared to be holding back the tide, keeping numbers in check at the same time as making a reasonable living from rabbit skins. However, during the Second World War most of the men enlisted in the armed forces, meaning that little rabbiting was done. The rabbit population increased so much during this time that after the war it was necessary to introduce well-organised destruction gangs. The summer of 1949 saw the formation of the Forks, Hawea, Lindis, Wanaka and Cardrona Rabbit Boards. One of the most difficult areas to control was the 272,000 acres (110,074 hectares) that came under the Lindis Rabbit Board. Although the large numbers of men who were employed killed so many thousands of rabbits that £12,000 was recovered from skins and carcasses, the rabbits appeared more numerous at the end of the season than they were at the beginning.

A change of tactics resulted in less emphasis being placed on recovering carcasses and skins and more on actual extermination. The introduction of poison drops from aircraft (arsenic trioxidised oats and carrots as well as phosphorised pollard) came next. During 1953 the Lindis Board dropped 1600 sacks of oats and 550 tons of carrots, at the same time as continuing the usual ground-based activities of trapping, bulldozing warrens and the use of dogs. In the 1950s the virus myxomatosis was introduced, but its impact was patchy as it didn't spread well in the absence of fleas.

By 1957 this combined attack had resulted in the deaths of many millions of rabbits in the Lindis area alone. There was quiet celebration as pastures grew, and hills turned green for the first time in many years. One small problem was reported, though. Suddenly, there was nothing to eat the shoots of the briar rose, so this started to spread at an alarming rate across good grazing land.

In the 1970s and 1980s Max Snow was a member of the Rabbit Board, which met in the bluegums at Tarras on the last Thursday of every month, and several times in between. He looked forward to these encounters and Madge suspects the gin bottle came out, because rarely did he get home before 7.30 p.m. The rabbits were marginally fewer in those days, and with the abandonment of rabbit boards in the 1980s they are now totally out of control.

top
An early-model car navigates the Lindis Pass — rabbit-infested country — early 1920s.

bottom
A Booth Bros lorry ready to leave Morven Hills with its load of wool, 1920s.

Gold rush!

In March 1861 a team of road builders was working in the upper Lindis Valley when one of them, Samuel McIntyre, suddenly came across some small pieces of gold. A veteran digger, McIntyre wasn't entirely surprised — he'd been quietly looking for flecks of gold because he thought the country was similar to where he'd been mining in California.

THERE WAS A GREAT FLURRY of excitement after Jock McLean broke the news of the discovery when visiting Christchurch on business. The *Lyttelton Times* of 20 March 1861 duly reported:

> Some weeks ago a party of men, employed in road-making by the Otago Government, picked up some nuggets in the river Lindis . . . a tributary of the Molyneux, where they were engaged in making cuttings for the main road to cross. Mr McLean, on whose run the gold was found, saw some gold in possession of one of the men; it weighed about four ounces, and consisted of large water-worn nuggets, from the size of a grain of wheat, to that of a bean, and apparently of a very fine quality. The men were about to leave the Government work and continue the search for gold, but their rations were stopped until work was resumed.

With news such as this it was hardly surprising that gold fever took hold. Men from all walks of life left their jobs, bought sturdy horses, drays, tents, mining gear and supplies and, with little thought to the onset of autumn, headed for the chilly hills of Otago. Within the next two months over 300 gold miners braved the rigours of the Lindis Pass and established claims on the upper reaches of the Lindis River.

Edward McGlashan fuelled the fever when his account of the diggings was published at the end of May 1861:

> I arrived at the goldfield on Monday, the 15th of April, where I found about 75 men engaged in the exciting work of prospecting and washing on the Lindis Stream and its small tributaries . . . I found the diggers located in the first gorge of the Lindis, and the washing stuff, the gravel, on the banks of the river . . . The character of the rock in the Lindis is a soft blue slate, plentifully intersected with small veins of quartz, evidently the matrix of the gold; a pipe clay also exhibits itself on the banks of the river . . .
>
> The gold met with on the Lindis and Hawea is both nuggetty and scaly; nuggets of the size of

> horse beans have been found. Two men, Docherty and Falconer, who have been working together for several weeks, assured me they had averaged over an oz. per day each. I believe, however, they had been the most successful up to that time. I noticed some large finds by sluice washing; at the same time others were not so successful. However, the field will be soon more thoroughly tested, as experienced miners have since gone into the district with the necessary appliances for working it properly.

Another lively account came from Englishman Robert Booth, who spent a couple of months at the Lindis diggings during the winter of 1861. Crossing the Lindis Pass in the depths of winter was challenging enough without the frosty reception that waited on the other side. When Booth and his three companions eventually arrived at Morven Hills they were hoping to be able to stay a night or two in the welcoming warmth of a shepherd's cottage. However, when they arrived at the first shepherd's hut 'the occupant, a worthy Scotsman, informed us with regret that we would have to arrange for our accommodation in the open, it being as much as his place was worth to feed or shelter diggers. This was unpleasant news, as we hoped to have taken up our quarters in his hut that night after our severe camping out the previous four days.'

Run-holder Jock McLean's hard stance was somewhat puzzling because not only was it at odds with the treatment that other run-holders afforded the diggers, but it was also inconsistent with his fundamentally generous nature. However, as a veteran of the Australian goldfields, it is probable that McLean had learnt the wisdom of avoiding the endless demands that diggers could place on those who owned the land.

Spirits lifted the following day when Booth and his party eventually arrived at the Lindis gold diggings:

> After passing through one of the most beautiful of the Lindis gorges we found ourselves at the

> entrance of a wide tract of open and undulating country, almost bare of anything beyond short yellow grass, encompassed on all sides by hills which stretched away westward to the snow-crowned mountains. The extent of the open was from one to two miles square, and through its centre — or nearly so — the Lindis flowed in a rocky bed.
>
> Along the river and far up the downs on either side were sprinkled hundreds of little tents with their hundreds of fires and rising eddies of smoke. The banks of the river were crowded with men at work, some in the water, some out, others pitching tents or tending horses, some constructing rough furniture, cradles and long Toms for washing gold, hundreds of horses tethered among the tents or upon the open, and above all the suppressed hum of a busy multitude.

Food was always going to be a challenge. Booth and his party had left Dunedin well supplied with about 10 cwt [hundredweight, about 50 kilograms] of provisions ('flour, tea, sugar, salt, ship biscuits, a small quantity of spirits for medicinal use and tobacco'), but after a couple of weeks some items began to run out. At this point they started to patronise the two goldfield stores — one run by a Mr Hassing, the other by Messrs McLeod and Gibson. These establishments were firmly recommended by one digger: 'Provisions of every kind are very reasonable here: flour, 60s per cwt; beef, 6d; mutton, 10s. per quarter; sugar, 1s. per lb; butter, 2s. 6d. per lb; tea, 5s; tobacco, 8s . . . I would advise any intending gold-seekers to expend none of their cash in purchasing provisions and bringing them here, as everything can be had at the stores at a more reasonable rate than by paying freight, with the risk of loss, and detention on the journey in coming up.'

Booth and his companions had initially hoped to buy fresh mutton and beef, but soon found that cheap meat was a scarce commodity. Although Jock McLean was happy to sell fat cattle to the diggers, many considered the prices he demanded to be excessive and chose to buy supplies from further afield. However, McLean's reputation for meanness may be a bit unfair as other diggers were more than happy. On 26 June 1861 an article in the *Lyttelton Times* noted that 'A speculator brought up some sheep to the diggings, but the sale for mutton is so very small that the venture will not clear expenses, and it is supposed he will take the remainder away. Mr McLean sells beef at 6d, which is preferred to the mutton; in addition to the price you have to carry it six miles, but it is as excellent meat as could be wished for.'

The stores were all very well when the weather held, but once winter set in things became a little more difficult. Booth reports 'soon after we were nearly having a famine, owing to the stores themselves running short by reason of the drays conveying supplies having been snowed up in crossing the pass. McLean was applied to, but he refused, and it was fortunate for him that a caravan arrived before the diggers were actually in want.'

Robert Booth also described the tools of a gold digger's trade:

> The usual requisites for a digger are a spade, pick, shovel, long Tom or cradle, and a wide-lipped flat iron dish (not unlike an ordinary wash-hand basin) for final washing.
>
> The long Tom consists of a wooden trough or race, twelve to fifteen feet long and two feet wide; its lower end is fitted into an iron screen or grating, fixed immediately above a box or tray of the same size. To work the machine it is set so that a stream of water obtained by damming up a little of the river is allowed to pass quickly and constantly down the race, and through the grating into the box at the other end.
>
> The 'stuff' in which the gold is supposed to be is thrown into the race, where, by the action

> of the current of water, the earth, stones, rubbish and light matter are washed away and the heavy sand, etc., falls through the grating into the box. As frequently as necessary this box is removed and another substituted, when the contents are washed carefully by means of the basin. By degrees all the sand and foreign matter is washed away, leaving only the gold.
>
> The cradle is very similar to what it is named after, a child's swing cot. It is simply a suspended wooden box, fitted with an iron grating and tray beneath into which the 'stuff' is cradled or washed by rocking it by hand.

After setting up their long Tom, Booth and his mates worked from dawn to nightfall, spending long hours digging, cradling and washing the dirt in the hope of striking it rich.

> The final washing of the stuff was done twice daily, at noon and again at evening, and what an exciting and anxious operation this was! How earnestly the decreasing sediment was peered at to discover signs of the precious metal! How our hearts would jump with delight when a bright yellow grain was discovered, appearing for a moment on the dark surface, then more careful washing, with beating hearts and necks craning over the fateful dish as the mass got less and less, and then the sinking and disappointment to find that the day's hard work of four men did not bring us five shillings worth of gold!

Unfortunately for Booth, and practically everyone else at the Lindis diggings, the quantities of gold were generally so tiny as to be not worth the time spent in working for it. Booth elaborated: 'The land was impregnated with gold, but the difficulty was to find it in sufficient quantity to pay.' After two months on the Lindis, he and his three friends called it quits, sold off their gear, packed up their few belongings and headed back to Dunedin.

The remoteness of the area, the high cost of supplies and the opening of more lucrative fields (such as Gabriel's Gully, near Lawrence) meant most miners had left the Lindis area by July 1862.

GROWING UP AT MALVERN DOWNS

by Madge Snow

Hector Gibson comes to Morven Hills

Now the story of Morven Hills turns to me. In 1913, my father, Hector Gibson, and his partner George Henderson plunged in at the deep end and bought the Breast Hill run, and the following year added Morven Hills to their holdings. Hector was 26 years of age and had been mustering since he left school. He had been head shepherd at Morven Hills under R.K. Smith, before the 1910 subdivision.

HECTOR WAS BORN on 25 September 1889, in the old stone house under the bluegum trees on a small plateau overlooking the Waianakarua River just in from the main south road.

His parents (my grandparents), along with their eldest two children, had come out from Dalry in Scotland and landed at Port Chalmers in 1882. Four more children were born in New Zealand, including my father, who was the youngest. His father died in 1892, leaving his mother to bring up six children under the age of 12. She died at Morven Hills on 4 July 1933.

George Henderson was born in Naseby on 5 April 1890; being of a similar age, he and Hector were great buddies, almost like brothers. During their early years mustering on several North Otago runs they built up a friendship that was to last a lifetime. George once told me (after several drinks) that Morven Hills had cost them £29,000. When combined, the two runs (Breast Hill and Morven Hills) had an area of 51,000 acres (20,639 hectares) and were occupied under pastoral licence. There were 17,000 sheep and 900 lambs on them.

No sooner had my father and George signed up for the runs than they also signed up for the First World War. When George was turned down (I'm not sure why) it was agreed that my father should go to war, and that George should manage their two runs. My father must have been quite a character, as on enlistment he wrote his occupation as 'plumber'. He embarked from Wellington on the *Athenic* on 30 December 1916 and was away for two years. George was eventually accepted as a soldier. His embarkation date was 2 May 1918, on the *Balmoral Castle*. He was sensible, listing his occupation as 'sheep farmer'.

After they returned from the Great War the partnership was dissolved, and Hector and George each took a portion of the run. My father, along with his widowed mother and an older sister, Ann, went to live in the old McLean homestead at Morven Hills. Ann cooked and looked after the men, and although she never received any wages, my father realised the great debt he owed her and made provision in his will that as long as she lived she was to be provided for.

My father farmed Morven Hills until 1924, when he purchased Malvern Downs from one-time Morven Hills manager

R.K. Smith. The well-known Malvern Downs merino stud came with the station and he continued this. He imported stud merino rams from Australia and became very highly regarded as a breeder of merino sheep. He was also a keen supporter of A&P Shows and as one of the most successful exhibitors was awarded many trophies. He was so highly respected that he twice had the honour of judging at the Royal Show.

In the post-war years a frequent visitor to the district was Elsie Elizabeth Mackay, whose grandmother had a hotel at Skippers Canyon. It was on one of these visits that she met Hector's friend and partner, George Henderson. Romance blossomed and, in the middle of 1923, they were married in St Andrew's Presbyterian Church, Invercargill. They went to live on Forest Range, George's property in the Lindis, building a house directly opposite the old McLean homestead at Morven Hills.

In the meantime, Hector had his eye on a local girl who worked in the Tarras Post Office. Born on 30 May 1903, Eileen Madge Jolly was the eldest daughter of Edwin (b. 1878) and Charlotte Jolly (b. 1874), who had a small farm called 'Kotiti', near Tarras. Charlotte's parents, the Perriams, owned the Lowburn Hotel.

In order, I suspect, to be near his beloved, in 1924 Hector purchased the Malvern Downs property, which was next door to the Jollys' farm at Kotiti. His next prize was my mother, Eileen, who he married in Dunedin on 16 September 1926. From this union, my brother William Hector was born on 4 July 1928 and I made my entrance in the early hours of 13 February 1932, hence my middle name, Dawn.

The early years of their marriage coincided with the beginning of the Great Depression in 1929. I think it was hard going, but Hector wanted my mother to have everything. I have only fleeting memories of my father but my impression is that he was generous to a fault and a big spender. They had trips to Australia (ostensibly to buy merinos) and he bought a small house right on the coast at Karitane as well as a new car. He also indulged my mother with furs and diamonds. After his death in 1938, Mother was left to pay off the debts. She

My parents, Hector and Eileen, on their honeymoon in 1926.

did just that, getting on with it and never complaining.

When Hector died in 1938, wham, suddenly it all came to an abrupt end. According to my mother, Hector suffered from debilitating varicose veins. In the winter of 1938 he came down with a nasty cold which later went to his chest and turned to pneumonia. He was told to keep warm and rest up in bed. With no exercise and little warning, in the late afternoon of Monday 20 June, suddenly and unbelievably, he took a turn for the worse. The family could see him slipping away and with death appearing imminent, an urgent call was sent to Dr Harrison in Cromwell. Before the doctor arrived, my father had died from a blood clot — he was only 48.

I remember being led in by my Aunt Ethel to say goodbye to him. He was laid out on a bed in the back bedroom off the big lounge, dressed in a dark suit, and I found it bizarre (I remember to this day) that he wore a pair of black shoes. I expected to see him in bed. I am quite sure when you are six years old, death has little relevance. It is part and parcel of life. You accept it for what it is, simply because you don't know any difference. You move on.

I can well imagine the utter grief and despair my mother must have felt on that grey, sunless day in midwinter, however. She was totally devastated. When Max and I spoke to Mrs Carlsen, the housekeeper at Malvern Downs at the time of my father's death, she told me that Mother had neither the composure nor the will to attend the funeral service in the church. Unable to face the prying eyes of the general public, Mother asked that a second, private service be held in the home my father loved, and that's what happened. On a cold, grey morning our close neighbour, Mrs Jenkins, picked me up and, together with her daughters, Molly and Frances, we sat by the cowshed at the top of the hill and watched as the cortege solemnly wound its way up the main road to the Tarras cemetery. Mrs Jenkins looked after me for the day.

His obituary described Hector as 'a man of splendid physique and a kindly nature and most generous heart', and continued, 'it could be truly said that Hector Gibson was a "big" man in every sense of the word. Possessed of a pleasant

My father, Hector Gibson, 1916.

personality and genial manner he endeared himself to a host of friends in all parts of Otago. He was a man of the highest integrity whose word was his bond and he was exceedingly popular with all those with whom he came in contact.'

A Malvern Downs childhood

> You can have all the education you want, but first you must learn to cook.
>
> — EILEEN GIBSON

When I look back on my life, I realise the backbone of Malvern Downs and Morven Hills was my mother, Eileen. She was completely unselfish and more than anything hated fuss or people putting on airs and graces.

SHE HAD NATURAL DIGNITY, strength and courage, and always faced adversity head on. On 20 June 1938 she was 35, had two farms, two small children, very little money and a huge mortgage. In her grief, how easy it would have been to have sold one farm, maybe both, and opted for a hassle-free life away from the land. Thankfully, my father had adequate life insurance and this saved the farms from being sold from under her.

From 1938 until 1953, seven days a week, 52 weeks of the year, Eileen never had fewer than three men to cook for. My childhood memories are always of her in the kitchen cooking. As I was growing up she always used to say, 'You can have all the education you want, but first you must learn to cook.'

After Mother's younger brother Bill married Jill Lethbridge from 'The Point' in 1941, our maternal grandparents left their farm at Kotiti and came to live with us. Although Charlotte (we called her Char) must have been an enormous help to Mother, I found her very difficult. She was always finding fault and trying to correct my table manners: 'Use the butter knife'; 'Cut bread, break toast'; 'Sit up straight'; 'Chew with your mouth closed'; 'Don't reach in front of others'.

Our grandfather 'Pop' was a great storyteller. No matter who came to the house, his opening line was 'Have you heard this one?' And, as quick as a wink, Char would add, 'Not in front of the children.' He always told a story nevertheless. Pop was always whistling and singing 'I'm going to hang out the washing on the Siegfried line'. And how he loved band music. The Radetzky March was one of his favourites and there was hardly a day when I didn't hear him whistling it. He loved to go to the South Island brass band competitions, and always gave us a half-crown when he came home.

I suspect I have inherited my love of band music from my grandfather. Every Monday night a Mr Hull came up from Clyde to show pictures in Mr Shadrach's hall. They always ended with Sousa's march 'Stars and Stripes'. I can't remember the films, but I'll remember forever the music.

OUR HOUSE ON MALVERN DOWNS was a square box with a wide verandah running round two sides and bedrooms branching off the central hall. There were two living rooms, one each side of the kitchen. The only time we ever used the big one was when Mr Smellie, the manager of the Trustees Executors, came up from Dunedin once a year and we sat down to tea and cakes.

The kitchen was large, with an enormous rectangular table, two upright chairs and two backless forms on either side of the table. Until the mid-forties all the cooking was done on a coal Shacklock range. A large green steel box with a hinged lid sat quite close to the range. This contained the sugar as well as plain and self-raising flour. Mother made her own self-raising flour. She would cover the kitchen table with newspaper and then weigh out nine pounds (4 kilograms) of flour, six ounces (170 grams) of cream of tartar and three ounces (85 grams) of baking soda. I was allowed to sit with her and run my washed fingers through the great pile until it was thoroughly mixed together. Still part of the kitchen but around a corner, we had a scullery. Brown linoleum covered the floor. In the late 1940s Mason & Wales drew up plans and the kitchen was modernised — oh, the joy of a dishwasher!

The bathroom was tucked in one corner off the verandah, which meant we had to go outside to get there. That was comfort compared to the 'long drop' toilet, which was down a path, under a large silver poplar and overlooking the orchard. A nail on a wooden dwang held a string loop, through which were threaded squares of paper, usually from *Straight Furrow*, a magazine for the farming community.

As finances improved, oranges appeared on the scene. These provided twin benefits. We had them in our school lunch and, even better, we had soft orange paper folded neatly in a box in the long drop. I can honestly say I can't remember using toilet paper until I went to boarding school.

One of my grandmother Char's unenviable jobs was emptying the chamber pots. Early in the morning she would be seen with bucket in hand and towel over her arm, carrying out what she described as her 'slop' duty.

Opposite the kitchen door was a series of sheds. One of these was the wash-house, complete with wooden tubs and a copper for boiling up the clothes. A large fig tree spread itself in ungainly fashion against the wall. In hot summers fig jam appeared on the menu.

Next door was the dairy where the milk was separated and cream cans were stored. Preserves and jam were kept on a shelf here, along with a large brown crock in which Mother salted runner beans. There'd usually be a side of bacon hanging from the ceiling. On another shelf was a large tin which contained rendered fat to make soap. Standing alone, and separate from the wash-house and the dairy, was the meat house, a small square concrete building that sat under a tank stand as this was the coolest place to hang the meat.

The hen run was halfway between the woolshed and the house. Often when there was a drop in eggs I would be sent to scout round the elderberry trees to find stray nests. If I lay on my tummy I would sometimes find a nest under the hen run. Mother would always put these eggs in a bucket of cold water and then throw out any that floated. Norton's egg preserve was kept in a square kerosene tin with a wooden lid. Spare eggs were gently lowered into this and, when preserved, would be used for baking.

Parallel to the toilet was a line of almond trees which my father must have planted when he first bought the property. A path led through these trees down to the cow paddock and the byre where the milking took place. On the southwest side of the house was a seldom-used circular drive which branched off the main drive. This area was planted with old-fashioned trees and shrubs, laburnums, arbutus (the strawberry tree), rowans, lilacs, sumac and sycamores. My father had planted the circular bed with roses but over the years these had succumbed to drought and neglect. A short path close to the house was edged with old-fashioned flowers such as aquilegia, lily of the valley and cosmos.

On the front lawn we had a wonderful walnut tree which Dave Aubrey from Cattle Flat had given to my father. That tree had enormous walnuts the size of duck eggs. Such a treasure. Dave and my father must have been great mates because he often dropped in wild pork when he was driving from Cattle

The Jolly clan, 1970. Back: Stuart, Eileen (my mother), Vic, Bill, Ethel and Lottie; front: Nyra, Vida and Audrey.

Grandma Jolly's Plum Sauce

6 lb (2.7 kg) dark blue plums
3 lb (1.3 kg) sugar
1 tablespoon ground ginger
3 pints (1.4 litres) vinegar
6 level teaspoons salt
½ teaspoon pepper
½ teaspoon cayenne pepper
2 dessertspoons cloves

Boil all together till cloves float — at least one hour. Strain through a colander then bottle.

Flat to Oamaru. I faintly remember him arriving in a very large car and he always came to the small side gate.

It was a simple life. We were self-sufficient in most things: meat, milk, vegetables, eggs. In addition to the usual potatoes, parsnips, lettuces, beans, cabbages and carrots, the very large vegetable garden had a huge clump of rhubarb, an asparagus patch, and one pear tree. A large pit was dug in the autumn, sacks spread over the bottom, and the carrots and parsnips were stored there, covered with more sacks and piled high with dirt.

There was an even bigger orchard that adjoined the vegetable garden on the south side. This lacked water and the fruit was never of great quality, but we still had apples, peaches and apricots in abundance, as well as wonderful satsuma plums. Mother made great quantities of plum sauce every year — this was mandatory at every meal, though I do remember my grandfather insisted on Lea & Perrins Worcestershire sauce as well.

LIFE HAD A STRICT ROUTINE: washing on Monday (the clothes were always boiled in the copper and then put through a wringer), cleaning on Tuesday and baking on Wednesday. Friday was butter-making day. The Still boys milked the cows and separated the milk and it was the job of Mervyn Still to churn the butter. Mother always made enough to last the week. She was always in the kitchen, cooking.

Hanging on a post outside the kitchen door was a ploughshare which, when hit, clanged loudly and brought the workers forth. Our meals were always at regular times: 7 a.m., noon and 6 p.m. Occasionally the ploughshare was rung if there was an urgent phone call and the men were at the woolshed.

Our meals, like life itself, were simple. We had boiled mutton quite regularly — once the fat was skimmed off, the leftovers formed the basis of a delicious soup. In those days cabbage was cooked until it looked as if it had been shredded. Mother was a dab hand at meat pies and always made her own pastry. We always had a roast meal on Sundays and, occasionally, if the men had boned out a shoulder, we had colonial goose (stuffed sheep meat), followed by a steamed pudding. The one thing I hated was junket. It appeared regularly, especially in the summer, along with stewed fruit. I have never had it since. Semolina was another obligatory understudy in the culinary world.

Char did lots of baking. I can still see her sitting on a kitchen chair, beating up butter and sugar with her knuckles. She would utter a childish rhyme: 'First the oven, next the tin. Wash your hands and then begin.' It must have been in the late 1940s when we acquired a Kenwood beater — that would have made her life easier.

Rabbits often featured on the menu. They were delicious. We'd sometimes go rabbiting on a Sunday — one of the Still boys would catch a couple of the ferrets that were kept in a deep pit in the pine plantation next to the dam and put them in an old tea box, along with nets. When we came to a hole with obvious signs of rabbit activity, the boys would lift a ferret out of the box and send it on its way down the hole, while at the same time putting a net over the hole and pegging it to the ground. Next there would be a great rumble and whoosh — out would pop a rabbit! The first would get entangled in the net, but if there was more than one, the second was usually lucky enough to escape. The rabbits were carried home in sugar bags, dangled from long string loops hung from our shoulders. They were skinned and cleaned then left overnight in the dairy in a large basin of cold salted water before being cooked with bacon.

Looking back I can understand why we had such simple food. It was peasant food, most of it; healthy and wholesome. With seven or eight people around the kitchen table seven days a week, my darling mother simply never had time for gastronomic delights. In her busy life, the old adage 'keep it simple' was necessary for survival.

LOOKING BACK ON MY early life, I now realise that there was a great emptiness after my father died. We were cared for, well-fed and loved, but there was little money for extras. We did not have social outings like other children and I can't remember Mother buying books. Any journals that came into the house were farming ones. Lucy Bell, a local girl, came for a couple of days twice a year and made clothes. I got a new frock once a year. I can't remember having a skirt made. Another local girl, Elsie Gillespie, helped Mother during this period. I was very impressed because she'd lean on the bench and kick out her legs; I thought she was tap dancing although she assured me it was nothing of the sort.

Bill and I rode our bikes three kilometres to the local Tarras School. When we rode past Mr Shadrach's shop (later the garage) his pet magpie would fly out and attack our ankles — I was terrified! Mr Colin Griffiths was the head teacher, with a Miss Dunmore as an assistant. We had to sit for hours learning how to write properly.

Young pines had just been planted on the boundary and all the pupils had to carry buckets of water to keep them alive. We had no swimming pool, but once a week we walked up the lane to the homestead of Mr and Mrs Jenkins and swam in the government irrigation race. Two pupils came from the head of the lane, Jean and Mavis Munro. Each lunch they had the biggest Red Delicious apples I had seen. I don't remember the schoolwork, but I do remember the apples.

We grew up with the Still boys, who were to remain part of my life for many years. Cliff, the eldest, came to Malvern Downs on 2 January 1948, aged 16, and returned there 30 years later after coming to Morven Hills with Max and me. Next came Ray, Mervyn and Les Still. Mother loved them all. She took them under her wing like a broody hen and they repaid her handsomely by being great workers. They had ferocious appetites and there was never any food left over;

Mervyn, with his big toothy smile, saw to that. One year there were seven Still brothers working in the Tarras district.

Holidays were rare but I remember going once to the beach house at Karitane. Mother's sister, Aunt Nyra, came with us. There was a clanking front gate and drifting sand right up the steps. The china was fine with a distinct brown pattern, almost like a Maori motif, running round the edge. The need for petrol coupons, and the desire to raise cash, meant the house was eventually sold.

Is it my imagination, or were the winters much colder then? A storage dam in the pine trees at the top of the rise used to freeze over regularly and we learnt to ice skate on the cold winter evenings. It was great fun, especially when we had 'skating parties' with a drum of burning wood to keep us warm. It was always a highlight when we were taken on a drive down to the Manorburn Dam at Alexandra and allowed to skate to our hearts' delight. That was very special.

I remember little of the war years. Managers came and went. There was a shortage of labour so land girls made an appearance on farms. Rationing started — we had coupons for food, clothes and petrol. Fat was rendered down and sent away to make soap. Housewives did up food parcels for the local men who were overseas and people picked rosehips from the roadsides; these were sent away to a factory and processed as a source of Vitamin C. Religiously, at 6 p.m. every night, the family gathered round the radio. We could barely hear the announcer through the crackle: 'This is the BBC World News.' Occasionally Winston Churchill delivered a sterling message to bolster flagging morale.

BILL WAS SENT OFF to Waitaki Boys' High School in Oamaru in 1942 and in 1945 I was sent to board at Craighead, a private girls' school in Timaru. In those early years I went by Mount Cook bus to Omarama, through the Waitaki Valley

top
Mother receiving the trophy for winning the 'Mother's Race' at Craighead in 1945.

bottom
Mother presenting the cups in my last year at Craighead, 1949. Miss Oakeley is to the right.

and on to Morven, where all passengers had to transfer to the train. This was a performance fraught with peril as the train stopped for no more than three minutes. I could barely lift my large suitcase so it was always a struggle to get it up from the platform and into the carriage before the train left. After a short ride to Timaru, the performance continued in reverse.

Judy Hyde, a pupil from Long Acre in the Lindis Pass, also caught the bus, along with Pat Munro from Rugged Ridges. Once in Timaru there'd be a taxi ride up Wai-iti Road to Craighead. We felt like little lambs taken away from their mothers.

I loved boarding school. I was lucky to be there in the period of Miss Mary Oakeley's reign as headmistress. She was English, young, vibrant and a strict disciplinarian. Mostly she wore her academic gown, but that aside, she wasn't known for her sartorial elegance and could be relied upon to have a run in her nylons or a hem hanging down. But it was her personality that shone through. She instilled in us the concept that girls can do anything.

The years passed very quickly. I never visited home during a school term, probably because of petrol rationing. We certainly never rang our parents, but I did write home every week. Sunday afternoons were set aside for letter-writing.

In 1948, at the afternoon tea after the school sports day at Labour Weekend, Miss Oakeley surprised my mother by asking the two of us to come and see her in her sitting room at the end of the day. My mother turned deathly white. She thought I was about to be expelled or something equally forbidding. I assured her that I hadn't broken any rules or been rude to any of the staff. When we were seated on the Sanderson-covered settee in the headmistress's office, Miss Oakeley turned to my mother and said, 'I'm going to make Madge head prefect next year.' My mother was speechless and I was stunned too because it was the first I had heard of it. Miss Oakeley finished our meeting with a brisk, 'That will be all, have a safe journey.'

As each boarder left school for the last time, on their final Sunday night they were allowed to choose their leaving hymn.

Miss Oakeley would introduce the hymn, and nine times out of 10 the girl in question would burst into tears. For my leaving hymn, I chose 'Abide with Me'.

I was so grateful my mother had sent me to Craighead. My days there were happy and fulfilling.

A new world opens up

In 1950, with my school days completed, aged 18, it was back to Tarras and the farm. Back home, I applied to do dental nurse training in Wellington and was accepted. However, Mother had other plans. With wool prices booming, and unbeknown to me, she was arranging an extended trip overseas, taking me with her. I can't have been too set on becoming a dental nurse as I recall being quite happy to do a world tour instead.

IT WAS THE FIRST TIME I had left New Zealand. We sailed from Auckland on the *Rangitata* at 5 p.m. on 19 May 1950. There were hundreds on the wharf, streamers galore, and a brass band which broke into 'Now is the Hour' as the ship slowly glided out to sea. Our cabin was filled with telegrams and exotic flowers.

Seven days later, our first stop was at Pitcairn Island, where we anchored and the islanders came out in boats and scrambled up nets dangled over the side of the ship with bags of fruit. The next day all the officers changed into white uniforms, including shorts, and the lounge furniture was draped in summer fabrics. Nineteen days later we reached the Panama Canal. My lasting impression was of how green all the lush growth was, a bright, iridescent green. No one stayed in their cabin as we watched, fascinated by the efficiency of the locks, one gate opening, another closing.

Most days we walked the decks and played shuffleboard or deck quoits. Partnered by an Englishman, I won the mixed doubles, and was presented with a pewter mug by the captain at dinner. We were travelling first class and there were several wool buyers on board. They and their families had the outside cabins.

Exactly one month after we left Auckland, on 19 June 1950, we disembarked at Southampton. We motored through Hampshire and Surrey to London, then carried on up to Scotland. When we were next in London the press gave a hint that Princess Elizabeth was due to have her second baby, so we trotted over to Clarence House. It was fortuitous. First came the Earl of Mountbatten driving on his own, and then (by all the cheering) we could tell the Queen was coming to visit her daughter. She sat upright, looking marvellous in powder blue, but never smiled nor waved. She looked concerned and there was no word of a birth.

We decided to go back again the following afternoon. We took the tube to St James and walked back to Clarence House. We'd been there only a short time when the big wooden gates opened and out came the Queen. This time she was charming. The car slowed almost to a halt. She beamed a big smile and waved to all, left and right. Instantly the crowd knew a baby had been born so we all cheered madly. Then at a second-floor window a blind was unfurled and, with a nurse holding him,

21-month-old Prince Charles, dressed in white, waved to the crowd. Shortly after this a policeman pinned the bulletin on the iron gates, breaking the news: a princess had been born.

Four weeks melted into each other as we bussed from one country to another: France, Italy, Austria, Switzerland, the Rhineland, back to France and Scandinavia. Back in London we met up with Mother's cousin, Doug Jolly, over a luncheon date. When Mother mentioned she was keen to buy a dinner set Doug drove us to a huge china shop where she purchased a Spode eight-piece setting, white with a gold edging. She also bought a nice silver standing cross for the Tarras Anglican church.

Doug also took us to the Hospital for Tropical Diseases, as it was necessary to have a cholera vaccination before we could fly home with British Airways. In 1950, flying from England to New Zealand took nearly a week. There were 37 of us, 10 women and 27 men, on an R.M.A. Charles Kingsford Smith Constellation plane with a crew of 10. First stop Rome, then a night in Cairo, then stopovers in Karachi and Calcutta before another night's stopover in Singapore. Then it was on to Jakarta, Darwin and Sydney. The last leg of the journey was by flying-boat back to New Zealand. We arrived back home in October, five months after our departure.

These travels opened my eyes to the world, and set the scene for many more adventures. I'd had a wee taste of the world outside New Zealand, and my itchy feet have remained with me ever since.

IN 1950 IT WAS WONDERFUL to see New Zealand's green and pleasant land after five months away, but doubly so to be back home again. I was eager to catch up with Max Snow, a friend who was manager at The Point, John Lethbridge's mixed property at Tarras. Max had written to me in my last term at Craighead, ostensibly to forward a few photos, but also expressed the hope that we would meet up in the Christmas holidays. When I told my mother, she had immediately suggested I invite him round for Sunday dinner. Remember, we always had a roast on Sundays. In the scheme of things, there was a little bit of match-making.

If I am honest, I have to say it was love at first sight when I first met Max. With his dark hair and healthy olive complexion I thought he was very good-looking. So I was keen to see Max again and to see if the sight of him still made my heart beat faster.

Born at Clyde in 1926, Max was the son of the railway stationmaster. His parents were both Scottish — his mother, who was born in Glasgow, never lost her accent. When the family moved to Mosgiel after his father's early death, Max went to King's High in Dunedin and then to Lincoln College in Canterbury. Max was delighted when he was appointed manager of The Point in 1947. Not only was this a great job, but his wage doubled from four to eight pounds a week.

I was impressed by Max's perfect manners. Always a gentleman, he never walked in front of me, always walked on the outside of the pavement, stood up when a lady came into the room, opened doors for me at all times, consistently asked what was to be done and, I suspect, when his time came, requested if he could leave this world.

After I returned from our overseas trip, Max became such a regular Sunday guest that Mother must have been eager to encourage the friendship. He used to turn up in a funny little truck; I have no appreciation of cars so I can't tell you what it was. Quite often it broke down so on two occasions he rode over on a horse. I was very impressed. By 1953 we were quite serious about each other. Unbeknown to me, Max (then 27 years old to my 21) arrived early one Sunday, cornered my mother in the kitchen and asked if we could become engaged to be married. Mother countered with a surprise of her own — she asked Max if he would like the position of manager at Morven Hills. Everything was falling into place.

In the meantime, my brother Bill was courting Frances

Jenkins. They became engaged first, with the knowledge that he would take over the management of our home property at Malvern Downs. They were married in the Tarras Presbyterian Church on 22 August 1953.

Once Bill and Frances were running Malvern Downs, Mother bought a house on Grey Road, Timaru. It fell to Max and me to get her packed up and moved over. Mother was not materialistic in the least so all her possessions fitted on the deck of a truck. The bulkiest of items were two brown leather chairs which my father had bought at the time of their wedding in 1926. I was given instructions to never let them out of the family so they have been covered many times and are in continual use here in Wanaka, where I now live.

Once Mother was settled, I moved in with her and found work as the receptionist for Dr Thodey, the Craighead school doctor, until my wedding day five months later. I am sure I secured the position because I was an old girl of the school. The time went by very quickly and on 26 February 1954 Max and I were married in St Mary's Church, Timaru by the Reverend Stanley Hurd. The reception was held at Timaru's Grosvenor Hotel. It was a small affair with about 80 guests at the celebration. We spent our honeymoon on the West Coast visiting the glaciers and then headed back over the Lindis Pass to begin our life together at Morven Hills.

From left: Philippa Ward, me, Jillian Grimmer and Margaret Gallagher on my wedding day in 1954.

The honeymoon years

In March 1954, as Finland and Germany officially ended their state of war, Max and I were busy unpacking and discovering the peacefulness of Morven Hills. We were so lucky. Max had already spent 12 months on the farm, learning the ropes. Now he was anxious to put his stamp on the property. We were the proud custodians of four horses, four dogs, two cows, one cat, a flock of hens and 9000 sheep.

THE MORVEN HILLS POPULATION totalled six people, us included. George Martin lived in a stone hut down in the willow trees adjacent to the derelict cookhouse. Through the cow paddock and across the road lived Father's old friend

George Henderson and his wife Elsie, along with their son Jackie, who was born with Down syndrome.

George Martin, Jackie Henderson and the Mt Cook bus were our lifeline to the outside world. When George periodically walked through the cow paddock with a black Gladstone suitcase, we knew it was to collect his regular liquor supplies. Jackie, on the other hand, would religiously meet the Mt Cook bus twice a day, at 11 a.m. and 2.30 p.m., and collect the highly anticipated *Otago Daily Times*. The driver would also drop off our mail bag in the morning twice a week, and collect it in the afternoon to take it through to the Tarras post office. Jackie also had the job of finding out how many people on the bus wanted afternoon tea; Elsie would then ring the tearooms in Tarras with this vital information.

I loved the peacefulness at Morven Hills. We were far enough off the main road to barely hear the traffic, and sometimes in the stillness of a summer's evening we could hear the running water of the Lindis River.

Shortly after I was married, I had such a sore back that it was an effort to make the bed. But that all changed when I read an article on a man who took magnesium salt to counteract ill health. I bought a packet of Epsom salts (magnesium sulphate) and mixed up a brew — one tablespoon in one pint (600 ml) of boiling water. I bottled this and started taking a small glass of this potion every morning, before anything else. I have been doing that for over 50 years. It unsettles the bowels for a few days, but they soon come right.

In those early days, all the farm work was done on horseback. But there were so many chores to be done before you could even think about working on the farm! The horses had to be fed, the cows milked and the hens given their scoop of wheat. In winter, we had an old pot on the coal range in which all the vegetable peelings were boiled up, a handful of mash was thrown in to thicken it, then it was delivered to the hens as a daily treat.

The job I hated the most was washing the separator each morning. All the cups were so greasy that it took lots of hot, soapy water to get them clean, before they were stacked up in exactly the right formation. One bucket of milk yielded a small jug of cream; it was so plentiful we had whipped cream with pikelets, scones, sponges and always with dessert.

Max taught me how to milk a cow; his recommended technique was to burrow your head into the cow's ribs, just like putting down a scrum. This approach meant I had to strain the milk before pouring it into the separator bowl. No matter how careful I was, there always seemed to be a cow hair floating inexplicably in the bucket.

I was never a typical farmer's wife, whatever that is. I never had a dog, never helped on the farm, and only gradually learned the names of the dogs and horses. My domain was the kitchen. To me, the kitchen is the heart of every home. Mother said, 'Feed the men well, look after them and they in turn will look after the farm.' They were very wise words.

All my life I have worked happily in the kitchen; I found I could be so creative. We always had puddings and during the winter months I played a little game to see how many weeks I could go without doubling up. With all the preserved fruit, sometimes I could stretch the variety out to three months. Luckily Max loved steamed puddings, and milk puddings as well, so it wasn't too difficult.

I never got tired of cooking, although I did get rather exasperated trying to control Dirty Dora. Cooking on a coal range is a real art; thankfully the hens were rather partial to food enveloped in burnt charcoal. Occasionally Max would catch me out, though, and say, 'A bit early for gardening, isn't it?' The coal range was great for ironing, though; I had a couple of Mrs Potts irons which were heavy metal with a detachable, insulated, wooden handle. They sat on one side of the range until needed; they're now antiques.

A new house and a new family

When Mr Neville, the manager from the Trustees Executors in Dunedin, made his annual visit to Morven Hills in 1956, he said he had looked at the books and thought it was time we built a new house.

THE IDEA TOOK US completely by surprise. We were so naive that, rather than building something substantial, we settled on a small, ordinary house from a book of plans. After a few enquiries we found Alwyn Keane, a Wanaka builder who was prepared to travel the 60 kilometres to the Lindis on a Monday morning and return to Wanaka late on Friday afternoon. Alwyn had a great team of men working with him, including Doug Jackson and Ken Smith.

But where to put the house? I wanted it to go on the flat below the cattleyards, but Max in his wisdom asked me to think where all the work took place. I said I knew it was round the shearing shed; 'So that is where it should go!' expounded Max. We argued back and forth until eventually Max won. We decided on a flat platform near the woolshed, just over the river from the old house. After it was built I was so thankful he had won that argument. A house on the flat would have been stupidity in its purest form because it was so far from where most of the work happened.

The next few months were very busy as I had to cook for the builders, but I loved it; when we had the men working there I knew it was all in the name of expansion and progress. There was always such a wonderful camaraderie. We had no electricity, but Gillies from Oamaru had installed a generator in one of the back sheds. It was turned on when I wanted to use the washing machine, which incidentally was installed in a tin shed down a concrete path with a long-drop loo attached to one end. It was a cold walk in the winter. We used Tilley lamps for reading at night. These felt like pioneering days.

By 1957 we had been married three years and though we had had fun trying, there was still no sign of the pitter patter of little feet. When I went to see Doctor Gilling, I suggested that perhaps we should think of adopting a child. She agreed and said she would look into it. She didn't have to look far because before long, I had to call on her for advice about morning sickness.

It was at about that time that we received a call from Cliff Still, who was working at Malvern Downs. He and Doreen Mackay were about to be married at Easter, he'd heard that we were building a new house, and would there be a position for a married couple? We jumped at the opportunity. I'd grown up with Cliff at Malvern Downs and I knew what a conscientious and hard worker he was. There was only one catch — Alwyn didn't think the new house would be ready until the end of May at the earliest. 'No problem,' we said, 'come on up and we'll all live together in the old house.' As it turned out the new house took six weeks longer than planned as a kerosene heater exploded in the hall when the painters were on the final stretch. The floorboards were so badly scorched that they had to be replaced and the smoke damage in the bedrooms was horrendous. Mind you, it could have been much worse. We could have lost the entire house.

We moved into the new house on 9 July 1957 — a very cold day with snow on the ground — and Cliff and Doreen finally had the old house to themselves. The new house felt like an iceberg. It had a Shacklock stove in the kitchen and fireplaces in the living area, but with no curtains or carpets it felt as unwelcoming as a crematorium. Gillies installed another generator in the woolshed, but it was turned on only for urgent duties, definitely not for heating. Luckily I had a big, thick Harris tweed coat which I threw on every morning and wore all day. It was a double blessing. We had lots of callers, and when they saw me with a jacket on they'd invariably say, 'Oh, you're going out.' Depending who they were, I would either agree or tell the truth. Rather naughty I know, but it worked a treat. I kept warm and drafted off those who were just rubber-necking.

In those days we were on a party line; I think our ring was a long and two shorts. Bargour, Forest Range and Breast Hill were all on the same line. It was a very light, flimsy line and the least bit of wind put it out of order. There were times when it was out of order more often than working.

The builders had left me a concrete block on which I put the clothes basket when I was hanging out the clothes. Every Sunday morning Max would take his shoes out and, sitting on the block, clean them. He was very fastidious about clean shoes, fanatically so; in fact it became a family joke. He would judge everyone on the state of their shoes. Later in the day he cleaned the car.

It wasn't long before we had a trip to Timaru and bought up large in the shop of Carter Joseph in Stafford Street. Owen Joseph was wonderful to deal with; a charming man of small stature, very fair and very helpful. He took a genuine interest in our requirements and even drove up to the Lindis so he could get the feel of the house. Our carpets, curtains, chairs and table all came from his shop. He became a true friend and, along with his wife Ida, spent many nights with us at

Morven Hills and, in later years, in Wanaka.

Once the house was decked out we set about laying out the garden. We had no agricultural equipment, but Max borrowed a tractor and plough from the Hendersons, cultivated a large piece of land and then built a fence around it. I had my heart set on a tennis court and suggested it was important to set one out before we planned the garden. Max would have nothing to do with it. He reminded me we'd had a big expense with the house so a tennis court could wait for a year or two. Subsequently he made a proviso: if I agreed to pay for it, he'd help with the work. When I asked Alwyn Keane how much it would cost, he quoted £395 for a concrete base so I said, 'I'll pay, let's do it.' I still have the receipt from 19 October 1957. It was such an asset and we had many hours of fun and entertainment.

DOREEN AND CLIFF STILL, the married couple, settled in well. Max called to see George Martin every day and probably Cliff did the same. Jackie Henderson still walked through the cow paddock with a gift of his mother's delicious yeast buns, and every six weeks Doreen cut my hair. She'd take a kitchen chair out onto the lawn, wrap me in a sheet and snip away. That was wonderful because if I'd gone to Cromwell for a haircut it would have been a major trip — 60 kilometres there and 60 kilometres back. We were able to savour small and simple things. It was such a peaceful setting, undisturbed as we were by the hustle and bustle of the modern world.

Doreen and I came to a working arrangement that she would give the men morning or afternoon tea if they were working on her side of the river and I would do the same if they were on mine. All the sheep work was done on my side, and all the cattle work on her side. Doreen also cooked for any single men who were employed (over the years, there

The avenue of silver birches that leads from
State Highway 8 to the house.

were quite a few). This worked wonderfully well and we had no arguments.

Both Doreen and I continued to do our cooking on our Shacklock ranges. Max was very good. He rose at 6 a.m. every morning and always got the fire going, which kept the house warm. We bought a fridge that ran on kerosene, but it had such a ghastly smell that it gave everyone a headache, so we had to consign it to the back porch. Finally, on 22 September 1959, the power was switched on in the Lindis. It was incredibly exciting at the time. We could vacuum, use the washing machine and the Kenwood, boil a kettle and do away with all the Tilley lamps.

IN THE INTERIM Doreen and I were in the production line ourselves. To our great joy I gave birth to Bronwyn Anne on 9 March 1958 and three days later Doreen produced Nancy Margaret. By the end of September 1959 we had two children each: Richard Gibson Snow on 30 June and Linda Mary Still on 25 September. Geoffrey Owen Still was born on 1 February 1961 and Peter John Snow made an appearance on 2 April 1962. Doreen outdid me and went on to have Robyn Anne on 19 December 1965.

Doreen was a great seamstress. She made all her children's clothes from Enid Gilchrist patterns. They came with an illustration and measurements, but she had to draft the patterns, and change them to fit. She always took a notebook when she went to town, and would sketch the styles she saw on the racks in the shops.

Each year, Max's mother always came and had a week with us. Glasgow-born, she had a delightful Scottish accent which she clung to fiercely. She entertained the children by taking them for 'picnics'. Best of all, I had a pillowcase set aside in which I stuffed all the clothes that needed mending: shirts that had lost a button, a collar to be unstitched — yes, we turned collars in those days — and all the holey socks waiting to be darned. This wonderful lady filled in her days by working her way through the pillowcase and seeing that all the mending was taken care of. She was a slight woman but worth her weight in gold. She was also very generous. Knowing we lived on lamb or mutton, she always came with a roast of beef. She died on my mother's birthday, 30 May 1985, in her eighty-eighth year.

NOW THAT WE HAD a new house the Trustees agreed that a cookhouse and men's quarters were urgently required. Up until then shearers and crutchers had always bunked down in the old stone buildings. They never complained but it must have been jolly uncomfortable for them. Back came the builders and another round of cooking. Again they came from Wanaka — Ken Smith, Ken Galloway and Craig Still, all under the leadership of Doug Jackson — and I fed them from Monday to Friday. The men's quarters were in a fine long-building with lots of bunk rooms off a verandah, next to the woolshed, with the cook's bedroom off the kitchen; and a long-drop toilet at the far end. It was a mighty fine building back in 1961 and we were very proud of it. I bought yards of cotton material and made curtains for all the rooms.

Max wasn't big on presents, but a few years down the track he asked me what I would like for Christmas. We'd left our hens behind at the old house, so I told him nothing would make me happier than a henhouse. Max ordered a big wooden one from mid-Canterbury and it was back-loaded on one of Radford's wool trucks. I was ecstatic — it was the best Christmas present I ever received! We placed it behind the implement shed, near the pine trees for shelter. Max cut a swathe of grass across the paddock to make a pathway and Maurice Kissock, a fencer from Taranaki, helped erect a fence to make a run. Bronwyn wouldn't have anything to do with hens, she appeared to be allergic to feathers; Richard wouldn't either — he appeared to be allergic to the thought of the hens. But thankfully, Peter loved them. He became the hen man. I loved them too. From time to time I'd walk over after lunch and open their gate so they could forage in the dump or in the pine trees.

In the early sixties, my mother had a few health problems and I could see that she might have to come and live with us, but with three children our bedrooms were full. The next time the Trustees came up from Dunedin they agreed we could build an extra wing. In 1965 back came the builders — Doug Jackson, along with Ken Smith, Keith Capell and assorted others. We pushed a wall out, put a carport on the other side and built a private suite around a snuggery and a new office. The additions balanced the house and made it look more presentable. One of the brickies, Monty Wright from Dunedin, offered to build me a wishing well in the garden. Whenever we went out on the hill we'd return home with a load of flat stones and he used these to build the lovely creation at the bottom of the garden. Juggling builders and three small children was quite a feat but I had lots of help from our Karitane nurses, such as the wonderful Linette Rowley and Eleanor Shaw.

One more piece of news about Mother: on 7 March 1967 she surprised everyone by announcing she was going to remarry. No fuss nor fanfare. I was shocked and asked for a brandy. Mother was 64 and had been a widow for 29 years. Her groom-to-be was Harry Purvis. He and his late wife Frances had been storekeepers at Tarras and Mother had known him all her life. We'd known him all our lives as well — we already called him 'Uncle Harry'. Harry was not what you would call a ball of charm. He was a bald-headed, cantankerous and tetchy old man. Still, he was good to my mother and they enjoyed each other's companionship for the next 19 years.

AT THE BEGINNING OF 1980, Dutchman Dirk Gootjes, who was then head of the Trustees Executors in Dunedin, read my father's will and then suggested that we separate the legal structure of the two properties. For 42 years, since 1938, Morven Hills and Malvern Downs had been run under the umbrella of the Estate of H. Gibson, and he felt it was time we went our own way. The Trustees established relativity between the respective beneficiaries (Bill and me) and it was agreed that Morven Hills should pay Malvern Downs $39,628.50 in cash in order to maintain the equilibrium of the two properties. The deed was signed on 21 June 1980.

LIFE AT MORVEN HILLS

ORION

Daily life in the high country

There was always someone calling in for morning tea, lunch, afternoon tea, dinner, or on exceptional occasions all four — that was part and parcel of high-country hospitality. It was one of my idiosyncrasies to always have a kettle boiling on the stove. This was a hangover from the Dirty Dora days when the kettle sat at the side of the Shacklock and was always singing.

BRONWYN, RICHARD AND PETER all had quite different personalities as children. Peter was scholarly and serious, not given over to making fun, whereas Richard had a tremendous sense of humour and a splendid gift for repartee. He was the family clown. Bronwyn was down the middle and never caused any anguish. All three were fun to grow up with and we had lots of laughs, usually at Richard's expense.

During my letter-writing sessions on Sundays, I would always type out the menu for the coming week and put it on the fridge. I could rely on the boys to cross something out, like a casserole, and replace it with a request for fillet steak. Wishful thinking!

Housebound for so many months with young children, my constant companion was the radio. A vital link with the outside world, it kept me in touch with what was going on. Max would turn it on as soon as he got up at six and it went all day long. Aunt Daisy was a real personality in those days; at 9 a.m. she would begin the day with 'Good morning, good morning,' and then proceed to tell her listeners what she had seen or done the night before, and you always knew what the weather was like in Wellington. Never lost for a word, she could talk at length on any subject. Several years later Sharon Crosbie took over and she became my all-time favourite. I hung on to her every phrase; a journalist whose articulate voice was matched by a superior intellect. Her diction was crystal clear, and her enunciation was so good that you heard every word. Listening to her was just magic.

It was a wonderful morning's programme and I hated going out of the kitchen in case I missed something. First up a band interlude would set the morning rolling, followed by devotions with ministers of different denominations reading from the Bible, and then a hymn. Every Thursday Sharon would interview Alison Holst, another New Zealand icon. The two of them discussed recipes, answered questions and constantly sparred with each other. It was pure pleasure to listen to them.

We used Sunday morning radio as a way to keep the family in bed longer so we could have a lie-in. I'd regularly write to Invercargill radio station 4ZA with requests for their children's programme. Week after week we heard the same tunes: 'Puff the Magic Dragon', 'Flick the Little Fire Engine', 'Sparky and the Talking Train' and 'The Lone Ranger'. The children would come running down the hall shouting, 'Did

George and Elsie Henderson with their grandson
Russell Emerson outside the Tarras church.

you hear my name?' In those early days I am sure that half the excitement was hearing their names called over the radio.

I have always loved the *Otago Daily Times*. Each year on a certain date they would have a joke trying to fool the readers. According to my diary, in 1982 on the front page they showed a photo of a Rolls Royce car being unloaded at the Dunedin chief post office, announcing it was the first of a new fleet of postal delivery vehicles; it was very convincing until you looked at the date — 1 April. On the same day, postal charges rose to 24 cents a letter. However, that wasn't a joke.

Because we didn't have television and Malvern Downs did, we often had Saturday night meals at Malvern Downs during the winter. My brother Bill and his wife Frances were generous with their hospitality and always invited us to watch the test games when the All Blacks were playing. It was only black and white but we loved being able to watch the games. Max was a great All Black supporter and couldn't get enough of the sport.

During the winter months we often went across the road and spent the evening playing cards — usually 500 — with George and Elsie Henderson. One week they would come to us and the next we would go to them. George loved a good yarn and, depending how much he'd had to drink, he usually ended up talking about my father. 'He was my best mate,' he would always say. I learnt so much on those winter nights. He said Hector had the biggest pair of hands he had ever seen; and as for counting sheep out of a pen, not a soul could match him. A thousand was no trouble and he was seldom wrong. I asked George how he did it. He said my father always wore a waistcoat, counting at the beginning with all the buttons done up; as he reached 100 sheep he undid a button, 200 another button and so on. Once he had five undone, equalling 500 sheep, he then began the procedure in reverse, so after he had undone and then redone the buttons, he had counted 1000 sheep. He then put a stone in his pocket.

George had a long-held dream to own a Chevrolet car so, after one of the wool sales, an agent took Max and George to Cook Howlison in Dunedin and George made the purchase.

Max drove it home. He was quite sure George and Elsie had their money secreted away in a biscuit tin, buried under the privet hedge. Any time they had to pay for anything, Elsie had to go outside to retrieve the money and the notes were always damp.

CROMWELL WAS THE HUB of our universe and we'd have a day there when it was necessary for farm business or if we needed a dentist's or doctor's appointment. Cromwell was such a small town that, as my grandfather used to say, you could fire a rifle down the main street and not hit anyone. The children loved going to the butcher's shop; they always hoped that Mr Bell, affectionately known as 'Ding Dong', would give them a saveloy. He'd turn to the great string of them hanging down at the back of the shop, cut off three and hand them over, saying, 'I know your mother doesn't feed you.' We always bought fresh sausages, saveloys and mince. He'd take the pencil from the back of his ear, write down the price with a great flourish on the brown paper, grab some string from a ball that dangled from the ceiling and wrap up the parcel.

Next we'd troop across the street and buy ice creams in Mr Roberts' tearooms. You could buy clothing items from either Mansor's drapery shop or, if you crossed the street again, London House. A little further north there was Mr Cox, the chemist, and up the stairs you'd find the dental surgery of Dick O'Kane. He was a much loved, charming man so you didn't mind going to see him. He'd fill your mouth with all kind of gadgets and then ask, 'Are there many quail in the Lindis?' He was a hunting, shooting, fishing man. Across the street again was Stumbles' general merchants.

Wright Stephenson's stock and station agency had a small office below the butcher's shop, but most of their agents were stationed in Alexandra where their main office was. They were our stock and station agent by choice and their agents were always thoughtful and considerate. The head man was Ian Scott, who made regular calls, but there was a succession of agents: Bob Long, Alan Bland, Alan Barber, Dick McArthur, Graeme Cambridge, Ron Burt, Lewis Pagan, Nug Dowling, Stuart Creighton . . . I'm sure I've forgotten some. I remember Dick McArthur's first mission was to buy guinea pigs for the children.

If they were coming up to the Lindis the agents would always ring ahead of time to see if we needed any groceries; equally if Max needed parts urgently he would give them a buzz and nine times out of 10 they rearranged their day to deliver the goods. I always knew to put an extra potato in the pot when one of them was due. The agents would take Max to wool sales, Hereford bull sales in Southland or even the occasional rugby match, and in the early days an agent took him down to hear Jesse Owens speak in Dunedin at the Sportsman of the Year dinner. They were all fine young men.

WE OFTEN HAD A family holiday in Queenstown at the end of January. For one week I didn't do any cooking. Each morning Max would take the children down to the local bakery and let them choose what they wanted for lunch. Cream buns and donuts were always popular, while Max was addicted to the custard squares and an occasional lamington. At night the Badcocks, Bonnie and Douglas, who lived on Frankton Road and became great friends of ours, would often invite us for delicious barbecues, or we'd eat at a restaurant or have fish and chips. For country children this was a really big deal! We all loved it. Sometimes, this week off was the only holiday Max would have all year.

On our way home after these short holidays we crossed the Clutha River on a short concrete bridge, at right angles to the Lowburn Hotel. We always stopped to pick up four cases of Moorpark apricots from Webbs' orchards and two

Picnicking with the Badcock family, 1967.

cases of Wiggin peaches from Mallett's orchard north of Lowburn. Apricots were Max's favourite fruit and I always made 5 kilograms of apricot jam and preserved the rest. Because most of the farm work was out on the hill the men usually took their lunch at least a couple of days a week. For months on end, by choice, Max had apricot jam and cheese in his sandwiches; they never varied and he never tired of them. Cliff, on the other hand, never ate jam — he was happy with Vegemite.

Apricot Jam

6 lb (2.7 kg) ripe apricots
6 lb (2.7 kg) sugar
juice of 1 lemon
¼ cup water

Stone the apricots and cut into quarters. Place everything in a large pot and bring to the boil, stirring frequently. Watch carefully that the mixture doesn't stick to the bottom of the pot.

Boil for 20 minutes then remove from the heat. Add a knob of butter to remove the scum. Bottle.

As long as you use equal quantities of apricots and sugar you can't go wrong. The riper the apricots, the nicer the jam.

School days

Schooling was always a difficult issue in the back country, and we were no exception. We were 30 kilometres away from the township of Tarras and the primary school. When we approached the Education Board to see if they would agree to fund a bus for the Lindis they came up with a suggestion — they would supply a bus, provided we found a driver.

SURPRISINGLY, THERE USED TO BE a 'household school' at Morven Hills, from 1914 or 1915 until the end of 1916. At this time it was customary for the Education Board to provide teachers for remote areas, but for classes to be held in a building provided by the local community. On 13 January 1915, the *Otago Daily Times* advertised for a teacher for the

Morven Hills household school. The salary was stated as being £6 a pupil and seven pupils were guaranteed. Classes were run in the small stone, single-roomed cottage that had seen service as the Morven Hills post office from 1864 to 1880. Miss Jessie Wishart, the teacher who took the position, resigned just one year later, and the school closed at the end of December 1916 when numbers declined to an unsustainable level.

For the first year of our children's schooling, we turned the cook's bedroom at the cookshop into a schoolroom and our daughter Bronwyn and Nancy Still had correspondence lessons under the guidance of local teacher Denise Wills. From that point we boarded either the school teachers or someone who worked in the local store, and they would drive the school bus in to work. From memory our first teacher/driver was Anne Middleton from Northburn, Cromwell (Northburn used to be one of Morven Hills' outback stations in Jock McLean's day). I remember Anne well. The minute she walked in the door, on would go a Jim Reeves record; how she loved his music.

I'm not sure in which order they followed, but there was Merin Cowie from Cromwell, who married an antique dealer, Robert Burton, and who now lives in Nelson. Her brother Colin Cowie was principal at the school from 1967–68. Davida Simpson from Lake Tekapo married Guy Mead and they live at the Dingleburn Station, Lake Hawea. Next came Richard McKay (1971), who I've lost touch with. We boarded two girls who weren't teachers but were lucky enough to get work in the local store. They were Mary Palmer and Patricia Kilgour. Mary married Neville Harris and lives in Wanaka; Patricia married a French chef, Claude Baudet, and they live in Whanganui. They all lived with us for a year and became part of our family.

As a backstop Max, who already had his heavy-duty licence, sat his passenger licence and was able to step in at a moment's notice. He in turn persuaded me to swot up all the rules and regulations, and in 1970 I too gained my passenger-service licence. Although I drove on the odd occasion I found it a real pain as it took an hour in the morning and another in

The old cookshop (top) and schoolhouse
at Morven Hills.

the afternoon, so I'd be driving along thinking of all the other things I could be doing. But the young people were delightful, and you learnt quickly that with children there are no secrets.

In 1964 Hector Bell, the chairman of the Tarras School committee, rang to speak to Max. He'd just been to Albert Town to see his good friend Murray Ellis and who should be staying on their land, camped on the banks of the Clutha, but the Hillary family from Auckland. Hector had bailed up Sir Edmund and persuaded him to come over to Tarras and speak in our little hall to help raise funds for the school. What did Max think? Max said, 'Grab him with both hands and don't let him out of your sight!'

Sir Edmund and Lady Louise came over to speak to the community on Saturday 4 January 1964. The hall was packed to the rafters, with standing room only. It was a fantastic night. Sir Edmund came on the stage all primed and bursting. He spoke about the epic climb and the reception that followed in Kathmandu; about hiring his suit from Moss Brothers and George Lowe dressing him; the panic of trying to find a large safety pin to take in a tuck at the back of his waistcoat (he was very thin) and finally his audience with the Queen. He had us all in fits of laughter and left the stage swinging an imaginary umbrella. The wives of the committee provided a supper plate for the official guests, so we duly retired to the kitchen, ate well and had a drink or two. Lady Louise was charming and merged effortlessly with the residents. We couldn't believe our luck.

AT THE BEGINNING OF 1970, we sent Bronwyn, aged 11, off to my old school, Craighead, in Timaru. With my mother living just round the corner it suited Bronwyn well because she was able to pop round at weekends and have lovely home-cooked meals.

Richard went off to boarding school during the first week

of February 1971. He went to Waihi, which is an Anglican preparatory school for boys, located just north of Temuka on State Highway 1. A small school functioning mainly for boarders, it had countrified grounds and a lovely family feel. Anyway, off we went through to South Canterbury with a suitcase of regulation clothes, all newly marked with Cash's name tapes. The closer we got, the quieter Richard became. When we arrived we were shown his dormitory. He was the first boy there and I think it had another three beds. Richard sat on the bed, looked out the window and then began to cry. I sat down beside him, put my arms around him and said, 'You'll be fine,' and at the thought of losing him to high school, I began to cry too. Subsequently, Max sat down beside me and he began to cry as well. It would have made the funniest home movie you could imagine. It was just too awful for words. It was a big learning curve for the two of us: make your goodbyes snappy and no lingering. Poor Peter; when his turn came in 1972, I think we said goodbye at the gate and never went near the dormitory.

Peter missed Richard dreadfully and pleaded to go to Waihi, but he was only 10. It was too young. If I had my life over again, I would never send my family away at such an early age. Mind you, living in the back country, sometimes you have no option, and it all depends on the circumstances. I firmly believe home life is the best for bringing up families. I can still hear my boys bounding off the school bus, bursting through the kitchen door and asking 'What's for tea, Mum?' It was a daily cry and made cooking a pleasure.

A couple of years later we went shopping in Ballantynes and picked up Richard's uniform for Christ's College in Christchurch. Richard had four years there and found it insufferable. Peter, on the other hand, went in 1975 and loved it. In 1976 the school fees for boarders were $622 a term, and for day boys $291.

When we drove to Christchurch for Peter's breakup at the end of the year, his housemaster told Max that Peter was too clever to go farming. Max was furious. He said, 'You have to be bright to go farming!' He was really angry. If we'd had any more sons, I don't think he would have sent them to Christ's College.

In 1979 Peter went off to Telford, an agricultural college in South Otago. He did well at Telford. His name went forward for a scholarship at an English agricultural college. A few of the boys had to go to Wellington to be interviewed and we were so excited and proud when we heard he had been chosen to study at Berkshire College in England. The scheme was sponsored by Overseas Containers Ltd, which meant he travelled over and back on a container ship. He left from Lyttelton on 15 July 1980 on the *Flinders Bay*, and was away for a year.

top
Peter, David Badcock and Richard at Waihi School, 1972.

bottom
Max delivering Peter and Richard back to Christ's College, 1976. The boys unpack the all-important tuck boxes.

Musterers and shearers

Our life at Morven Hills revolved around sheep. Their needs ruled our days. I never worked with the sheep directly — my job was to feed the workers. It was a job my mother had trained me for, and I loved it.

WE HAD ONLY BEEN at Morven Hills a month or two when, one Sunday morning in April, we were lying in bed discussing what work had to be carried out before the end of the month. Max said they'd be going out mustering in six weeks' time, about the second week in May. The May muster signals the changing of the seasons as it's when all the stock is rounded up and brought down to lower levels before the snow coats the tops of the mountains. When Max said they'd be gone four to five nights I asked him to run over what food had to be prepared for the four men. I still have his list in my recipe book:

- √ cooked leg of meat
- √ tin of mince
- √ tin of fat
- √ tin of stew
- √ chops
- √ saveloys
- √ sausages
- √ tin of peas
- √ black sauce
- √ butter
- √ salt
- √ milk
- √ plum pudding
- √ fruit cake
- √ potatoes
- √ tomato sauce
- √ bread
- √ eggs
- √ beer
- √ apple shortcake
- √ fruit loaves

'What about a brass band?' I asked.

'No,' Max answered in all seriousness, 'they'd frighten the horses.' He didn't even laugh.

Truly, it was a logistical nightmare getting all the food ready for the autumn muster. All the food had to be packed into two wooden kerosene boxes which were then loaded into the saddle bags that rode on either side of the oldest and biggest packhorse. In those days golden syrup came in very large tins so I put the eggs in one empty tin, surrounded them with sawdust, and then replaced the lid. It was important that the boxes were both the same weight, so the horse remained balanced.

Before we even got to this stage, the horses had to be brought in so that their hooves could be inspected. The old smithy was the left-hand building in the yard. Max would fire up the forge after he'd milked the cows in the morning and Aubrey May, the farrier, would spend his day repairing hooves, removing old shoes and replacing them with new ones. It was fascinating to watch Aubrey work because, contrary to what I imagined, all the new shoes had to be hammered into shape. One size didn't fit all.

Whenever Aubrey removed an old shoe, he'd trim the horse's hoof. Then he'd remove a new red-hot shoe from the forge and place it over the hoof so he could compare the size. The smell was hideous. This done he'd move to the anvil where he'd hammer and chisel away with great precision.

In May the sheep were mustered.

Once he was satisfied with the fit, Aubrey would drop the shoe into cold water. When it was sufficiently cool he then nailed it onto the hoof. It took all day to shoe all the horses and was hard work.

It would be interesting to know how much Aubrey was paid for this back-breaking labour but I never found out. Max was very chauvinistic in that regard. I was eager to help with the bookwork, but in all my years at Morven Hills, I never once signed a cheque. Max insisted he was the boss. I didn't give it a lot of thought — it was just the way it was, and I really was happy in my role running the kitchen. I saw it as the engine room of the family and the farm. I really loved making sure everyone was well fed, which in turn made the farm tick over nicely.

THERE WAS AN AIR of excitement as the day of departure for the muster loomed near. All was ready: the food, the horses, the dogs, the men. All we needed was for the weather to co-operate, as the task needed four fine days to complete. Every night, Max sat glued with one ear to the radio for the latest weather forecast. 'Please, no rain.'

Once the forecast was clear, there was pandemonium as the musterers gathered in the yard. The horses were jittery, with at least 20 yapping dogs sniffing every fence post, snarling and eager to be off. Max gave me a quick kiss and off the pack trotted down the drive, heading for the Dip Creek hut where they'd spend their first night. Dip Creek was so named because in Jock McLean's day the sheep were dipped there before they were shorn. During the musterers' two days at this hut, they'd round up the mobs and then move them to a paddock nearer the homestead. They then rode further south to Polson's hut. This was their base while they brought the sheep off the cold, dark faces. They would then gradually drive them nearer the homestead.

On the fifth day, if the weather was calm, you could hear the ghostly sound of dogs barking as the mobs of sheep began to come over the hill. It was exciting to hear this far-away noise, so I always went out to the yard and listened for them. As they progressed down the hill and onto the flat I'd hear men's voices. Not so ghostly now — the air would be sprinkled with expletives as they controlled their foot-sore and worn-out canine friends. On a good day they would have a mob of 9000 sheep. It was exhilarating to see such vast numbers of sheep rippling down the hill, like tussocks waving in the wind.

The exhausted men, haggard, with five days' stubble and dry peeling skin on their faces, always made a beeline for the kitchen where, with a large bottle of Speights in hand, they sat around the table and had a re-run of how their dogs had handled the sheep. I'd listen to the stories as I unpacked all the empty food containers and gave them a good scrub. It made me feel part of the team.

It's not possible to farm this high country without a team of good dogs. They are an integral part of the high country. They all take years of training, but different dogs are trained to do different things. Some are taught to bring the sheep towards you and are bred not to bark (heading dogs), some to bark and chase the sheep away (huntaways), and 'handy' dogs do a bit of both. My favourites are the backing dogs, which run along the backs of the sheep in the yards, pushing them down the race and up into the shed. I always loved watching them; they got so excited.

Max had seven dogs, all with different skills. However, he'd sometimes have a couple that were trained to do the same thing. One would be a kind of insurance. When Max was out on the hill he couldn't afford to have a dog pack up because of sore feet or a dislocated joint, so he'd take an old dog and a young one, hoping it would learn. Max loved them all, but once they were back home they were tied to the fence and never allowed to come inside the garden.

MAY WAS ALWAYS EXCEPTIONALLY busy as much had to be achieved before the weather broke. The days that followed the autumn muster were given over to drafting the sheep. As they went through the yards, they were separated into different groups. The ewes went into one pen, the wethers (castrated rams) into another. Then both mobs were redrafted — this time so that the young and the old sheep could be separated.

At Morven Hills we kept our sheep for six years. After that the oldest were sold, usually after shearing, to a farmer on flat land further south, who would generally grow them on for another two years. Each six-year period was represented by a different-coloured ear tag, so the man on the gate had to be razor sharp and read each tag as the herd ran towards him. Occasionally, he'd give a yell, 'Oi, I've missed one!' When that happened a man would scramble into the pen, find the offender and throw it over the fence to the correct mob.

Crutching was the next big job. This meant bringing the whole flock into the woolshed. Crutching involved trimming the wool round the sheep's eyes so they could see the grass, then cleaning up all the daggy wool round their bottoms; 'topping and tailing' as it was called. During the 30 years we lived at Morven Hills, we always had the same gang to do the crutching in May and the shearing in November/December. Brothers Charlie and Frank Brophy were contractors from Timaru; Charlie organised the shearing gangs and Frank travelled with them. They worked on all the big stations and usually did a circuit from Otematata Station near Omarama to Mount Nicholas on the shores of Lake Wakatipu before coming to Morven Hills. Often Charlie had several gangs working at the same time. Frank was short and stocky, a lovable teddy bear. Whatever he told you, he always ended his sentence with 'Know't I mean?' Sometimes you did, and sometimes you didn't.

After crutching the mobs were put out on sunny faces, so

top
Peter in the woolshed
during shearing time.

bottom
Frank Brophy counting
the sheep.

that when the snow came, they wouldn't be without tucker for long. If they were kept at a lower altitude they'd cope with whatever nature threw at them. The ewes were put in the paddocks with the most grass and before the end of the month the rams joined them.

It was a relief to get to the end of May and realise that most of the stock work had been taken care of. The winter months were given over to maintenance. For a start, Max checked all the vehicles for anti-freeze and did bookwork. Cliff worked in the willows down by the river, cleaning up and preparing next winter's firewood. The pall of smoke round the old buildings was the signal that Cliff was burning the rubbish. I loved the smell of smouldering leaves and burning wood — that was the fragrance of autumn.

In the winter the men usually spent a week cleaning out the manure from under the woolshed. They used a sheet of corrugated iron with string tied to each end; one man was doubled over shovelling the manure onto the iron while the other man pulled it out and dumped it. It was a filthy, malodorous task and there were always lots of grumbles that week.

The men also checked fences and fixed broken rails in the yards. When Max rode out and checked the hill fencelines, he often took a packhorse loaded up with rock salt. The salt came in square blocks in a distinctive pink — the colour came from the salt's mineral content, including iron. The sheep had a healthy appetite for these blocks and so they had to be continually replaced. Max also put out salt blocks for the horses and the cows.

Born in the late spring, lambs were about four weeks old when it came time to mark them. Marking is the term applied to the procedure of earmarking, castrating and tail-docking the lambs. First the mobs had to be brought in and the lambs separated from their mothers. This was a distressing time, with much bleating and baa-ing. The lambs were lifted up with their backsides on the top rail and then earmarked (the tag would go in the left ear for males and the right for females) and docked. The docker would pull the lamb's tail tight and then, with one stroke of his pocket knife, sever it by cutting through wool, skin, muscle, sinew and bone. Each tail would be placed in the appropriate heap, males left, females right. This was very important because Max then knew exactly how many wether lambs he had to sell. A sheep's tail carries blood vessels so there was always a great deal of blood around. Quite often, especially with larger lambs, blood spurted out. As a result, everyone engaged in lamb marking got covered in blood. You couldn't help it.

The male lambs also had to suffer the indignity of castration. Would-be rams became wethers. Once the docker had cut off the end of the lamb's scrotum, he had to get hold of each testicle, pull it out, cut it free and then drop it on the ground. Squeezing the scrotum close to the sheep's belly usually made the testicle come into sight. In the early days some men did it with their teeth; Max had false teeth so did it with a knife. Cliff Still would collect the testicles in an ice-cream container and take them home for Doreen to cook in butter after she had egged and breadcrumbed them. They were quite a delicacy and went by the marvellous name of 'mountain oysters'. When you think about it, it's no different to eating brains or kidneys, just a different part of the sheep. Doug Still adored them.

I hated marking time. Once I went out to the yards to observe and once was enough for me. Never again. It was the worst job on the farming calendar. The men's clothes smelt to high heaven and they all had to be soaked and scrubbed. Suffice to say it happened every spring, but I won't mention it again.

Then summer would roll around. In those early days we always shore from the end of November right through to January. Shearing was the most important job of all; it meant a lot of work for everyone, as well as much frustration when bad weather struck. Max could get very tetchy at shearing time. It was fine when everything was going well, but when there was a change in the weather, or if the sheep weren't running well, we all got a 'round or two for a pound or two'. At times like this, I only opened my mouth to put food in.

Help came in the form of Jillian and Warwick Grimmer, two

young Christchurch cousins who for several years spent their summer holidays at Morven Hills. We had lots of fun. They both had oodles of personality and fitted in well with farm life. Without fail, Warwick arrived with one large suitcase plus a carry-on which had to be handled with the utmost care. Max and I were a little puzzled until we discovered that Warwick always travelled with his own private food kitty — a tin of chocolate-chippie biscuits and another of afghans made by his mother, with new supplies arriving every two or three weeks. I think he kept them under his bed. We teased him unmercifully but Warwick had such a wonderful disposition that our comments were like water off a duck's back. He always came back with a smile and a very quick response. His full name is Alfred Warwick, so several of the men got to calling him 'Afghan Alf'.

On the Henderson side of the road by the bridge that crossed the Lindis River, there were two corrugated-iron huts that housed a couple of rabbiters. Early one May when all the men were away on their annual muster, Warwick and I were the only ones at home. It was around 5 p.m. on a stormy Friday night and getting dark.

Warwick had just come in from milking the cows when there was a knock on the kitchen door. It was one of the rabbiters. He reeked of alcohol, slurred his words and had great difficulty standing. He asked to use the phone. They were out of beer and he wanted to ring the Lowburn Hotel to order a crate to come up on the Mt Cook bus next morning. I told him the phone was out of order, which it was, but he didn't believe me. The phone was through the hallway so I told him to follow me and he could try. He rang and rang to no avail. At that he became quite abusive and followed me back into the kitchen. I told him to sit down and I would make him a cup of tea. He didn't want to sit down, he didn't want a cup of 'bloody' tea; he wanted a bottle of beer. He was hostile and aggressive so I told him to go home and have a good night's sleep.

He turned around, opened the outside door, stood there swaying for a few seconds and then said in a very clear, loud

top
Drafting the sheep.

bottom
The sheep were sent into the shower dip after shearing.

voice: 'I am going home to get my gun and I'm coming back to shoot the two of you.' Poor Warwick, he'd been sitting on the seat under the window and hadn't said a word, but he was visibly shocked and so ashen that he looked as if he'd swallowed a dose of embalming fluid. As soon as we'd had tea he scuttled off to bed, and I could hear a lot of heaving, pushing and shoving, and squeaking on the linoleum. When I sang out and asked him what he was doing he told me he was moving his bed and every bit of furniture hard up against the door. I have to admit it was pretty scary. We were both very relieved when morning came. Nothing appears quite as alarming in daylight.

Shearing was a busy time for everyone, but especially so for the cook. We didn't have a cookshop during those first few years so the men, usually about 12 in all, trooped into the old house for all their meals. They all sat round the large table in the big room off the kitchen, smoking, yarning and putting the world to rights. I quickly learnt it was best to start preparing early, so at least six weeks before the shearers' expected arrival I began filling up the tins. Every day I made fruit cakes, fruit loaves or two or three kinds of biscuits. Being organised was half the battle. I guess it is the same with everything in life. By the time the men arrived most of the baking was done and it was a matter of cooking and cleaning, which, providing we had no hold up with the weather, went on for three to four weeks.

Before shearing we always placed a big grocery order with Wardells in Dunedin. Everything came in bulk: boxes of dates, boxes of sultanas, large tins of golden syrup, sacks of flour and hessian bags of sugar. I would unpick the seams of the sugar bags and make aprons. Women always wore aprons in the kitchen in those days.

This all seemed a lot, but it was nothing to the supplies that were required in the McLean era. On 31 March 1874, 10 tons of flour was ordered! In those days it seemed that men lived on little other than bread and mutton.

When the shearers were there we would eat a sheep a day. All the men had a chop and eggs in the mornings. Every

Shearers' Buns

6 oz (170 grams) butter
6 oz (170 grams) sugar
2 eggs
2 cups self-raising flour
pinch of salt
handful of sultanas
vanilla essence

Cream butter and sugar. Add eggs, one at a time. Beat well and then add dry ingredients, fruit and a few drops of vanilla essence. Place dessertspoonfuls on a cold tray and bake for 15 minutes at 200°C.

Back: Me, Max, Jillian Grimmer, Red Sharkey and Warwick Grimmer; front: George Martin and Lil Bowler. Christmas, 1956.

evening Max would cut off the required chops and I'd put them into the huge roasting pan that was the exact size of the oven. Before I went to bed I'd bank Dirty Dora with lots of wood, put the pan in and cross my fingers that by the morning the chops would be well cooked, succulent and delicious. I was a great believer in long, slow cooking, especially for mutton. In the middle of the day we would have mince, made from shoulders of meat with the help of an old-fashioned grinder which I screwed to the wooden kitchen table. In the evening there was more mutton — this time in the form of two legs roasted in the big pan.

Vegetables came from a Chinese family called Chang who owned a greengrocery in Waimate. Once a week, usually on a Friday, Mr Chang would put a box of fresh vegetables on the Mt Cook bus for us. He always picked out the biggest and the brightest of everything, and because we never knew what we were getting, it was like a lucky dip.

Smokos were always important. As soon as breakfast was finished, the cows milked and the separator washed, it was scone-making time. After scones I made sultana buns. The scones and buns went into the morning smoko basket and then in the afternoon I'd produce a fruit loaf, sliced and buttered, and a tin of biscuits. Every so often Jackie Henderson would come through the cow paddock bearing a batch of yeast buns from Elsie. I could have kissed her! She was incredibly kind to me. Muffins hadn't made an entrance in the culinary department at that stage but I could make an assortment of scones: sultana, cheese and, my favourite, griddle. An old griddle with its inverted U-handle sat permanently on the hearth. With a coal range I often made gems; ginger gems were a particular passion.

Access from the house to the shearing shed was by a picturesque swingbridge over the Lindis River, followed by a short climb up to the shed. The rouseabout always came down to get the food basket. It was his job to bring it back at night to have all the mugs washed. There was never a crumb left over.

For several years Max employed Mark Bennett, an

Australian, to class our wool. He lived with us in the house and we got to know him really well. George Martin helped out at the yards as well so I fed him too. On Sundays we always invited him up for a roast dinner. Because we had a surplus of cream we had it whipped every day with pudding. Max loved whipped cream. George always left the kitchen with his verandah-like moustache embroidered with a neat white edge. 'Yoose done good,' he'd say.

During the first shearing of 1958 I remember we had the most amazing cloud-burst. After two days of non-stop torrential rain, a huge torrent of water swept past our back door at the new house, through the garage, and then flowed into the storage sheds. It would have flowed through the house if we hadn't had concrete steps at the back door. Max rushed down and borrowed George Henderson's tractor and plough, which he drove while Mark steered the plough to make a dam with a wide furrow to guide the water away from the house. People probably wondered why we had a mound in a seemingly flat paddock, but it was very sensational at the time.

New Year's Eve was a big night for the shearers, and Max was always happier if they stayed on the farm. If they went away, we could never be sure when and how many would come back, or what state they'd be in. When they decided to stay with us on New Year's Eve 1956, we held a barbecue in the willow trees down by the river. Max contributed all the chops and ordered sausages.

The men wanted music so we got six men to manhandle the old piano we'd inherited onto our old Bedford truck and Max then drove it down to the bonfire. The night was bright with moonlight and excitement. One of the shearers, Barney, hopped up on a chair and played the night away. You name the tune and he could play it. To our amazement the old piano had a honky-tonk sound and under the stars it sounded great.

That group of shearers was amazingly talented. One chap had a guitar, while another made music with a couple of spoons and then started up an astonishing drumming rhythm on the back of one of my cake tins. Max loved to sing. He wasn't always in tune but he knew all the words of all the songs and was never slow at leading a chorus. They hoisted him up onto the back of the Bedford and, leaning on the piano, he launched into this Australian folk song:

> There's a track winding back
> To an old-fashioned shack
> Along the road to Gundagai
> Where the gum trees are growing
> And the Murrumbidgee's flowing
> Beneath the sunny sky . . .

This was too much for Fred, who wasn't much of a singer. Jumping on the truck, he shouted, 'I'll give you a real dinkum Aussie story,' and began reciting the Banjo Paterson classic, 'A Bush Christening':

> On the outer Barcoo, where the churches are few
> And men of religion are scanty
> On a road never cross'd 'cept by folk that are lost
> One Michael Magee had a shanty . . .

Although he was slugging on a bottle of beer, he was able to recite all 12 verses. A reverberating round of applause and whistles followed and Aussie Jim said, 'Come on, Fred, give us "The Man from Snowy River"!'

> MacFierce'un came to Whiskeyhurst
> When summer days were hot
> And bided there wi' Jock Macthirst
> A brawny brother Scot . . .

'You stupid bastard, that's not "The Man from Snowy River". Get off the bloody truck and I'll do it myself!'

> There was movement at the station, for the word
> had passed around
> That the colt from old Regret had got away

And had joined the wild bush horses — he was
  worth a thousand pounds
So all the cracks had gathered to the fray . . .

Each man tried to outdo the other; we had singing, recitation, beer and burnt chops. How Banjo Paterson would have loved it. When, in the small hours, Max declared 'game over' and time for bed, George Martin, having sat on a fallen willow log all night drinking John Bull stout, delivered his usual one-liner: 'Yoose done good.' It was a night we would all remember. For Jillian Grimmer it would be part of her higher education.

EARLY IN THE NEW YEAR, Max always went down to the home farm at Malvern Downs to choose his rams. Like crutching, shearing and lamb marking, this was a yearly event. He and Cliff Still kept busy trying to improve on genetics and building up stock numbers. Come spring we had pilots undertaking aerial oversowing, and fencers dividing large blocks of land. Then there was the usual cycle of work. Life followed a fairly established routine: lambing, tailing, mustering, shearing, dipping, mustering, crutching, fencing and so on. The sheep numbers continued to grow during the 1970s. As long as wool prices kept up, the drone of top-dressing planes filled the valleys in winter and spring; superphosphate was going out by the plane-load. In 1974 we shore 410 bales of wool. During the 1960s and '70s, the men worked five and a half days a week and had Saturday afternoons and Sundays off.

In 1963, Max turned the key that unlocked our high country. This came with our first Land Rover, purchased from W. Reid in Luggate. Buying the Land Rover was a giant step forward in opening up the hill country, as it greatly simplified the way things were done. As far as Morven Hills was concerned, it revolutionised farming. Horses were

In 1974 we shore 410 bales of merino wool.

gradually phased out but we kept a few which were used for cattle work. Max had started out running Galloway cattle but later switched to Herefords as he decided these were much easier to handle.

New roads were formed with abandon. Jack Young brought his bulldozer from Wanaka and spent several weeks mapping them out. In the spring he'd be back maintaining the old ones — and especially so if the winter had been severe. Within a few years you could basically drive all over the high country. It was exciting to watch the station develop and sheep numbers gradually increase.

New fencing was still being carried out and the larger blocks were becoming smaller and more manageable, which meant that it was easier to bring the sheep in at mustering time. Fences were often washed out during winter, so spring brought a continual stream of fencers. We often had Bill Cowie fencing for us. He was a local identity and a real character. A tough man of the land who was notorious for his fearless exploits and mishaps, his wry sense of humour and warm, generous personality endeared him to everyone.

Every autumn Max spent a couple of days at the bull sales. These months were always given over to cattle work, either weaning calves or testing the cows for TB. Max was always tense when he was waiting for the results to come through. It was such a relief if the readings were negative, but it wasn't always the case; those that tested positive had to be culled.

ARTIST COLIN WHEELER SPENT a week or so at Morven Hills in 1970, working on paintings for a book on historic sheep stations of the South Island. The book gives a valuable insight into how the station was run at the time. Colin wrote:

> Forty miles of access roads have made horses
> almost obsolete and have simplified management.

They are not five-star highways: they edge past terrifying drops, they slope disconcertingly towards the brink on blind corners, but they're a godsend. Mustering is done mainly by Land Rover, with access requirements providing many station owners with new roads, or upgrading old ones . . .

Today Morvén Hills shears 13,300 merinos with 4,200 breeding ewes. 'We produce 374 bales of wool, with an average fleece weight of ten pounds.' Max Snow laces his boots. 'Our rams come from another Gibson estate property twenty miles down the Lindis Burn, and managed by a son of Hector Gibson, who founded the Malvern Downs Merino stud in 1924. We do no cultivation and buy hay only for two dairy cows. Cattle? We run 270 Galloway cows, and bought 100 Hereford heifers and cows this year to control the surplus growth induced by oversowing.'

Max smiles when I mention shearing. 'It has been simplified by the use of a contractor. You know, $28.50 per 100 sheep with narrow gear. The contractor provides shearers, fleecies, classer, packers and a cook. We provide the food, the cook does all the meals and smokos. We supply the sheep — and the weather!' His voice trails off reflectively.

'Our rainfall is twenty-five inches, and tends to increase,' says Max as he adjusts the idling jet on the truck. 'As for snow, we're not in the danger belt, though about a quarter of our country can be unsafe in winter. Snow lies on the tops all winter, with at least one good fall at the homestead, which is fifteen hundred feet up.' Frosts of twenty degrees are common, and often reach thirty-two degrees. Despite the heat of the summers, the property is fortunate in having abundant creek and spring water for stock.

WHEN SPRING CAME you always thought ahead to shearing time. The station cookshop had to be cleaned out and made ready for the cook. You never knew if they'd be male or female; they were always a bit of a problem but that was the domain of Charlie Brophy, as he did the hiring and firing. I had to agree with Mona Anderson. In her book *A River Rules My Life*, she wrote that if you had a good station cook, you should keep hold of them and use them for breeding purposes. I could write a book about the cooks we had. Some lasted for years and others for one week.

Colin was one of my favourites, but he was not without his faults. He was an affirmed alcoholic, but although he had several binges, they never seemed to interfere with his work. I always cleaned out the cookshop after shearing and was astounded by the places I found gin. The white vinegar bottle, the almond essence bottle and the innards of the toilet were all favourite hiding places.

Colin loved a game of tennis and in the evenings he'd come over to the homestead and together we'd take on the shearers' team. Colin was a great slicer of the ball. Richard generally preferred to go shooting and was what I would call a basher. He loved to hit the ball over the fence. Peter played a lovely game and could clean us all up. Max played periodically, perhaps on a Sunday, but was usually so worn out during the week that he was happy to fall into bed. Unfortunately Colin was a smoker as well as a drinker and after a few years his health began to deteriorate. I was sad when his health gave out and he had to retire.

Hereford cattle.

Pets

One of the wonderful things about living a rural life is interacting with the many animals that cross your path. The children loved adopting stray animals and had a wide range of pets during their childhoods. Like all rural children they had a good understanding of life and death, the whole circle of life.

LIKE ALL FARMING FAMILIES we had our share of pet lambs; lambs that had lost their mothers and had to be bottle-fed. Usually they started out in the kitchen on a sack in front of the Shacklock range, and then as they got stronger they were put out in the woodshed in a box to keep them warm. You would hear them bleating through the day, reminding all the world they were hungry. When the children were young, we had one or two every year. We even took them to the Wanaka Show so the children could enter them in the pet parade. One year we were late arriving and missed the judging. The lake rose with the tears shed.

Max didn't think that pet lambs were worth all the extra work because they never rejoined the flock, and nine times out of 10 there would be floods of tears at the end of the day when something happened to them. On the other hand tourists loved them and always went into raptures over the 'dahling little things'.

Peter vividly remembers his first pet lamb. 'Skippy was a wether, a merino. He'd always come straight up to me. Young sheep — hoggets and two-tooths — were unaccustomed to going up the ramp into the woolshed, but if I had Skippy with me I'd lead them up no trouble.'

Peter always had pet guinea pigs too. He'd dig out clumps of green cocksfoot and throw it into the cage, and give them water and clean out the hutches. Unfortunately the dogs were quite partial to guinea pig if they could get into their hutches, but, like rabbits, there was always another litter on the way!

For Richard's ninth birthday, we bought him a blue budgie as he loved birds. He named this one Rusty, despite the fact that he was a pretty blue. Rusty's cage sat on top of the fridge in the kitchen and Richard gave him seed and fresh water every morning, but Mother was left to clean up the mess that he scattered with reckless abandon. I talked to him every day while the children were at school and was amazed how quickly he learnt to impersonate. Once he got one sentence he would repeat it over and over. 'Richard's a good boy'; 'Did you get the strap?'; 'Have you done your homework?'; 'Look out, Dad's coming!' I know the boys taught Rusty to say 'Bugger', because I certainly didn't but it popped out quite often. I thought, what wonderful company a feathered friend must be for someone sick in bed. Rusty lived for several years and then one morning we got up, and there he was dead on the bottom of his cage. We were all very sad.

One spring afternoon a few years later Richard came in after a day out on the hill with two tiny chickens, not much

top
Richard and his pet bird Rusty, with Peter and Patricia Kilgour, 1968.

bottom
Max and me with Charlie Winchester, the pet chukar.

bigger than large bumble bees, in his Swanndri pocket. He said they were chukars, a type of pheasant. We found a cardboard box, padded the bottom and sides with lots of old dusters and put it right on the outer edge of the coal range so it would keep warm. Richard hand-fed the chickens with very fine oatmeal. Next morning he was sad to find one had died, but remarkably, he hand-reared the other. As it grew feathers and put on weight it became very tame and was soon a family pet. This was in the days when the boys watched the American television programme *M*A*S*H* and they were greatly taken with one of the characters, Charles Winchester. Richard's little chukar became known as Charlie Winchester.

Just as I'd done with Rusty, I talked to Charlie all the time. He'd put his head on one side as if to say, 'I'm listening.' The first year, he seldom left the kitchen. The second year he would sit up on the bench or table when I was baking or working in the sink, follow me through to the laundry and sit on the tubs and then follow me all through the house. He loved it when I made the beds; I'd purposely pull the sheet almost to the floor and he'd pop in and out, as though we were playing games. The third year he ventured outside; whenever I went out into the garden Charlie followed on behind. If I was weeding and I got well ahead of him, I just needed to call 'Charlie' and he would fly over and land by my hand. He loved to dust himself in the dirt and hide under the foliage of the plants. His favourites were the pulsatillas, which he could squat under; their arching fronds were ideal for his game of hide and seek. Occasionally he'd pop his head out and there would be the odd squeak, as if to say 'Find me!'

As befitted his name, Charlie Winchester was terribly pompous and always preening himself. I had a routine where I'd go in about 5 p.m. to put the evening meal on and have a bath. He'd fly over to be with me, and side by side we would enter the house. I'd often try to duck in without him noticing, but he was too clever for that. He would fly round the house until he heard the water running and then he'd fly up on the windowsill and tap on the louvre windows until I let him in so he could sit at the end of the bath. In those days I subscribed to *Time* magazine and I loved to read it in the bath. Charlie would think he was being ignored so would start tapping on the bath. Eventually I'd put the magazine down and talk to him, and then he'd follow me to the kitchen. After the meal he established himself in the living room and usually sat on my shoulder and rubbed his beak through my hair. It was a lovely sensation.

After several months he realised that no one was taking notice of him any more so he began to get quite aggressive. When I put him down on the floor he'd get so annoyed that he began to pull tufts out of the carpet. When he did this, we put him outside. Then to show he was really, really angry, he would fly up to the dining room windowsill and tap, tap, asking us to let him in. We ignored him until he began pecking out the grouting around the windows with his sharp little beak. Like a small child, he wanted all the attention. Amazingly, we could even go away for a night, come home and call out his name, and he would come flying in. He was such a character. We all loved him. By the time he was four years old he was starting to fly further and further away. However, he'd always come home until one day he heard the call of chukar on the hill, and decided it was time to join them. Well, that is what we hoped had happened.

Most years we had dozens of magpies and I can't say I was rapt with their continual squawking noise. I hated them. In the spring the boys and Geoff Still would go bird-nesting. As soon as they arrived off the school bus, they'd have a biscuit and then go round the pine trees making a note of all the nests and counting the eggs but never touching them. Once they came across a magpie's nest almost at the top of a pine. When Richard started climbing up Mother Magpie became very aggressive and kept bombarding the boys in a terrifying manner. They did an Olympic sprint to the house and I could tell they'd had the fright of their lives.

When I lived at Tarras I had joined the Wanaka golf club and I continued to play during those early days of married life, practising in the horse paddock during the week. It was a long drive but I enjoyed the camaraderie and it kept me in touch with the outside world. Through this membership I became the proud possessor of an amazing legacy. In the late fifties I had the good fortune to win one of the golf club's Christmas raffles — a hamper. At the time I had no idea what was in it, but all was revealed a few days after the draw: a fruit cake, chocolates, shortbread, a bottle of gin and a turkey. I had a ring from Lillian Faulks at Mount Barker. She told me the Faulks family had donated the turkey and did I want it dead or alive? When I asked Max, with no hesitation he suggested we take it alive, 'and please, if it's possible, could we have a gobbler?' No problem. Within a couple of weeks we took delivery of a sugar bag, with the largest black head swivelling on a stretched neck poking out of a small hole cut in the side, investigating the landscape. Immediately he was christened Stewart, after Lillian Faulks's husband.

At the same time Max saw turkeys for sale in *Straight Furrow*. He rang the number and ordered two hens from a farm in North Otago. The turkeys bred at such an alarming rate that soon we had the birds all over the yard. From that small nucleus we now have literally hundreds of birds roaming the hills at Morven Hills. One Sunday I was sitting on the bed, having removed my nightie and peeping under the quilt for my underwear, when Richard came running down the hall and burst in, gasping in one sentence: 'There are five turkeys in the garden; gee, Mum, what big headlamps you've got.' He was nine years old.

Dogs were a vital ingredient of a high-country sheep station, but they were working dogs. Max had seven dogs, and we used to joke that I came eleventh in the family, after the seven dogs and the three children. If a working dog was injured or killed by a car on the main road, it was a disaster. Every working dog had a different role; some brought the sheep in and some chased them away. It would have been impossible to farm Morven Hills without the dogs.

We did have one dog, however, who didn't have to earn its keep. One Saturday evening, we were dining at the hotel in Wanaka with a group of friends when the wine waiter asked

Peter and his dogs.

Richard and Annabelle.

if any of us would like a Labrador pup. I was so relaxed after a glass or two of wine that I replied, 'Yes, we would love one.' Instantly I felt a kick under the table and looked at Max, who wore a thundercloud on his brow. I realised I was skating on thin ice so I quickly followed up by saying, 'We live in the Lindis, so sorry, we can't take it home tonight.' The waiter countered with the offer that he would love to deliver it next day. He had six pups and this, a bitch, was the last of the litter. He was desperate to find a home for it.

He triumphed. Next morning he arrived with a very small golden-haired pup, not much bigger than a man's boot. The waiter had his girlfriend with him, Annabelle, a very striking, slim blonde with cropped hair. Instantly, I said, 'We'll call the pup Annabelle.' She became one of the family, and Richard's friend, for several years.

Richard spent the next year working for Bill Jolly at Kotiti and spent all his weekends hunting with Annabelle. I was truly amazed at how intelligent she was. He usually arrived home about 1.30 on Saturday afternoon with a load of dirty washing, so every Saturday Annabelle would sit at the brow of the hill from about 1 p.m. waiting for him to come. How did she know which day of the week it was? When she heard Richard's car on the main road, she would start running down the drive to meet him. It was extraordinary. Richard would reach for his rifle in the gun cupboard and then ask, 'Will we go and shoot a rabbit?' She would jump up and down in little dance movements and then start howling with delight. There was great camaraderie between the two of them. Richard's bedroom had an outside door and once I caught him reading his gun magazine with Annabelle cuddled in under the eiderdown. I was angry and said, 'Richard, you know you're not allowed dogs in the house!' With a plaintive look he replied, 'Annabelle isn't a dog, she is one of the family.'

What could I say to that?

Gardening

I can't explain exactly why I love gardening so much; perhaps for me, it's proof of the hereafter. A plant can be absolutely had it, and then in spring it comes away again. I especially love growing things from seed — it seems a great act of faith to plant a seed in the ground and to wait to see what appears.

IN THE SPRING OF 1957, shortly after we moved into our new house, we planted silver birches down the drive and framed the paddock with pines. The months melted into each other. We were happy and blessed with sparkling, crisp mountain air and, as the song goes, the stars at night were big and bright. I planted hundreds of daffodil bulbs down the drive between the silver birches. At the same time I cut the centres out of the birches to make them branch.

Shortly after I started my garden Elsie Henderson gave me a very old plant which I have treasured all my life. 'Princess Mary', a very special blue viola, grew at the Skippers Hotel at the time it was owned by Elsie's grandmother. When Elsie married George on 27 June 1923, she made sure that Princess Mary came with her to the Lindis. It's a slightly clearer blue than 'Maggie Mott', but its real benefit is that it doesn't seed. You need to take new pieces off each spring to keep it healthy and growing, otherwise it becomes quite leggy. I've given it to all my friends and I am sure it has done the rounds in Central Otago. As the Americans would say, 'It is a dahling plant.'

Tom and Dorothy Goodger were our near neighbours, and Dorothy was a splendid gardener. We didn't see them very often but occasionally she would give me a ring after the country library van called and say, 'Come on over in the afternoon and choose some books.' From memory, she was allowed to borrow 30 at a time. Once I'd selected a few books, she'd ask me if I would like to take a few iris rhizomes and, in November 1959, I did just that. The Goodgers' grounds were ablaze with the colour of roses bursting into bloom and a rainbow of tall bearded iris along the driveway. When I said I would love some irises, and would be happy to get them after Christmas, she said, 'No, take them now.' She told me irises loved the hot, dry climate of the Lindis and that she was already a member of the New Zealand Iris Society.

When we went inside, we found Tom sitting in the sunroom reading the paper. Dorothy asked him to dig out some plants. 'Later,' he said. With that Dorothy leaned over and whipped the paper out of his hands and over his head. 'Now,' she said. And out he went . . .

I went back to Morven Hills with a bundle of books and a sugar bag of iris rhizomes, and never looked back.

Not long after this a notice in the *Central Otago News* advertised an inaugural get-together of iris enthusiasts in Alexandra. It was the middle of shearing so I rang, put in an apology but said I would definitely be interested. From then on I tried to attend all the meetings (only three a year), and

Iris 'Pacific Dawn'.

my garden increasingly bulged with irises. They were easy-care plants, required little attention and flowered abundantly. As long as you leave the rhizomes uncovered they will reward you with the most tantalising blooms. From that time irises overflowed from every corner of my garden, ran riot in Max's patch and spiralled all over in brilliant profusion. Immediately after they'd flowered I'd divide them and then take huge barrow-loads to the dump, but they had the audacity to grow and flower just as well there.

While I'm on the subject of irises, I should mention our Central Otago group. We had a great bunch of members, held together by our secretary, Eileen Forrest. Glad McArthur, who wrote a weekly gardening column for the *Central Otago News*, was a leading light, but Maryed Urquhart was the queen bee, so witty and knowledgeable. When we had the 1984 Iris Convention in Alexandra at the beginning of November I suggested we give each member a pound of butter to make into biscuits, to be eaten at the morning and afternoon teas. The butter was expensive but it was still cheaper than paying caterers to feed the 140 delegates. The variety was astounding. We had about 40 members so you can imagine the mountain of different biscuits that were produced. We elected a 'biscuit lady' to be responsible for selecting which biscuits were to be eaten on what days.

After a few years of iris meetings in Alexandra, I found myself on the committee and later became president of the Central Otago group. This led to a stint on the New Zealand Iris Committee and ultimately a three-year term as president of the society. This meant a lot of travelling and speaking to various groups.

I also joined the Scottish Rock Garden Society and loved getting their seed distribution — I used this to build up my collections. *Gentian acaulis* flowered prolifically and set seed all over the place. The seed is tricky. You have to watch it very carefully; the seed pods are vase shaped and the secret is to cut them before the autumn rains, or else they fill up with water and rot. When they were ready, I'd cut off the stalks with a pair of shears — I usually got two plastic buckets full of dry pods. I'd then put these in the kitchen blender and chop them up with the steel cutting blade. After the fine seed drifted to the bottom of the blender, I would sieve it and then throw all the chaff-like debris back over the garden. Word must have got around because I received a letter from Watkins Seeds in New Plymouth asking if I had seed for sale. I sold them large phials for several years and usually made over $100. That's a huge amount of seed.

Bulbs thrived in our climate. I was particularly fond of fritillaries. I had them coming on from seed each year. To flower a difficult bulb, seven years after sowing the seed, equates to ecstasy. They revelled in the dry summers and multiplied unbelievably. The only problem was the smell. *Fritillaria imperialis* must be the smelliest plant on the planet, smelling of skunk or rotten meat. One of my favourites is *pallidiflora*, which is lucky because it grows so easily, almost like a weed. *Pontica* and *raddeana* are other favourites, probably because they are green. I love green flowers.

Fritillaria imperialis was my barometer. When I saw their lime-green shoots peeping through the ground, usually during the last week in August, I'd know that spring had arrived. I planted this variety in rows, like potatoes, in Max's vegetable garden and sold several fruit boxes full each year to Parva Plants in Tauranga. Each one had to be wrapped individually because they bruise easily. From memory I received $1 each and now I see gardening centres selling them for $25.

When I put an advertisement for selling bulbs in the *New Zealand Gardener* one year the replies were overwhelming. I set up a trestle table in the garage and dealt with them in a very business-like manner. Some years I made over $1000 from seeds and bulbs. What a marvellous hobby for any housewife, I thought. If you can have patience for the first three or four years, then you have bulbs coming on all the time.

IN 1979 I READ of a two-day bee-keeping course being run at Telford, an agricultural college in South Otago. I made up my mind I would do it, put a line through the days on the calendar that I would be away and off I went to Balclutha. Peter had started a course at Telford that year, but he just ignored me. It's not the done thing to have your mother studying at college while you're there.

I enjoyed the classes. There were 17 men and three women. I didn't become an expert, but I learned enough to get started. I had to buy all the protective gear: white overalls, a hat and veil, plus a smoker and a small tool with a hook for lifting the frames. I bought two of each because I couldn't lift the hives on my own and would need the help of one of the boys. Max and Peter said they wanted nothing to do with bees, but good old Richard offered to help. I purchased four hives and I was away. I put them in a sheltered spot behind the implement shed, on the way to the henhouse.

In the spring, as soon as pollen is available for feeding the larvae, the annual cycle of growth begins with a rapid expansion of the brood nest. Bees are fascinating — they are such intelligent little critters. They only work at a certain temperature and all hives are totally dependent on their queen. In the winter they gather round to keep her warm, and in the heat of summer they use their wings to fan her and keep her cool. You can hear the fanning noise as you approach the hives.

The instructor at Telford said to treat the bees like Plunket babies, to handle them gently and not get them agitated. I remembered that the smoker helps calm them down, so did what I'd been told and made the fire within, with hessian or pine needles. Richard always came when I needed to lift the hives. No matter how careful you are you can't help but get the occasional sting. It's an occupational hazard. It was interesting because Richard suffered hayfever but the more stings he got, the less of a problem the hayfever was.

The hives had to be registered and numbered, and a man from the Ministry of Agriculture in Oamaru came once a year to inspect them, usually in the late autumn. On one visit he asked me why I had so few hives. He thought I should have at least 30 to make it profitable. I told him it was only a hobby for my garden as I loved to grow plants from seed and the bees helped with the fertilisation. I told him how one problem plant, the pretty little blue Chilean *Tecophilaea cyanocrocus*, flowered profusely every spring, but never set seed. He asked me if I had two hats and veils.

'Yes, of course, because Richard helps me.'

'Well, the next time that crocus is in flower, put your veil on, bring your spare hat and veil over, lift one frame out, scoop up a handful of bees and put them in the spare hat. Be careful you don't scoop out the queen or you will have the entire hive after you. Then turn the hat upside down over your flowers. I guarantee you will get a seed head, if not several.'

I couldn't wait for September to roll round. At the end of the month, spring had sprung, birds were singing, daffodils embroidered the driveway, primroses abounded and the leaves of the silver birch were unfurling when, not to be outdone, the shy little *Tecophilaea* beamed with a dozen dainty smiles. The men were out on the hill with their lunch repairing a fence when I thought, 'This is my moment in time to play God.'

It was an unusually warm day, the kind when you shed clothes, but being quite contrary, I slipped into overalls, donned gumboots, hood and veil and walked over to the hives. With my gloves I scooped up a large handful of bees, put them gently in the spare hat, and then pulled the veil around them. I was in the middle of the paddock, midway between the hives and the house, when a red car came screeching up the drive. A man whom I had never seen before wound down the window and asked to speak to the boss. I told him to ring after seven that night. He asked, 'What are you doing?'

Truthfully I answered, 'I'm carrying bees over to the garden.'

'Struth!' he said, winding up his window and going down the drive so fast that you'd have thought he'd been stung between the legs. He never rang and I never saw him again. He's probably still dining out on a story that if you live in the high country for too long you become a bit loony.

The wishing well in the garden at Morven Hills.

Douglas Badcock paintings of mustering on the Morven Hills (top), showing Cliff Still at the front and Max Snow behind, and looking up the Lindis River (bottom), with the top of the stone woolshed showing to the right.

Tussock scenes around Morven Hills.

The Lindis Pass (State Highway 8), showing the Tarras side (top) and the beginning of the pass just after the turn-off to the woolshed.

The Lindis River. In the early 1860s gold diggers flocked to the upper reaches of the river, hoping to strike it lucky. One theory is that when the gold ran dry, many men were employed by Jock McLean to build the stone woolshed, house and cookshop at Morven Hills.

Pastoral scenes around the Morven Hills woolshed.

top
Morven Hills Station, showing, from left, the house, smithy, stables, schoolhouse and cookshop.

middle and bottom
The old smithy and Jock McLean's original house.

Inside Jock McLean's old house, after Annie Snow gave it a facelift. We lived here for four years before we built a new house.

opposite
With 'Dirty Dora', the Shacklock range, looking pristine.

top
Schoolbags that the men sometimes used to take their packed lunch in.

middle
In the kitchen: butter pats, kerosene lamp and bean slicer.

bottom
An old Singer sewing machine resides in the hallway.

There is debate about when the magnificent T-shaped stone woolshed was built, but it may have been as early as 1861.

The woolshed had two shearing boards and 34 stands for blade shearers. In 1908 it was reported that the greatest number of sheep ever shorn in one day at Morven Hills was 4812 — almost 145 per stand.

top to bottom
The old smithy, stable and schoolhouse.

The old cookhouse was built around the same time
as the woolshed.

Scenes from my Wanaka garden: geraniums at the front door (top) and marguerite daisies.

clockwise from top left
Iris 'Harbour Blue'; rose 'West Coast'; rose 'Golden Queen'; rhododendron 'Trude Webster'.

top
The family tree installed on the side of the Wanaka house.

bottom
In the Wanaka garden under the walnut tree.

I LOVED ALL FOUR SEASONS at Morven Hills. I couldn't say which one I liked the best. Before Christmas the lupins always raised their heads, jostled for attention and draped the banks of the river like a rainbow scarf. Often they brought the traffic to a halt. Then in summer the Morven Hills flat was covered with a prolific white daisy called an oxeye; there were acres of it and yarrow as well. I knew they were weeds but I loved them. Later in January the flats assembled glorious banks of blue as the viper's bugloss came to the party. I tried picking their furry stems and putting them in water but they didn't last.

Each February threw up an innocent-looking little yellow daisy, but innocuous it wasn't. Hieracium had arrived. I remember reading an article that called hieracium a creeping death in the high country, describing its spread as an ecological disaster that would make the rabbit problem seem insignificant in comparison. This plant is so invasive that it is virtually impossible for other plants to grow. It is thought it originally came in contaminated pasture mixes from Europe and first became established in New Zealand in the 1880s. By the 1920s it had been recorded on several lowland sites in Canterbury and by 1940 it was noticed in the Otago high country.

Up on the hill in the dry tussock-covered areas are numerous stands of *Aciphylla*. It's a grand name for the obnoxious wild Spaniard or speargrass. I am told the flowers are sweet smelling but I can't vouch for it. The sharp sword-like leaves are capable of inflicting painful wounds — it is a vicious plant and not one to be interfered with.

Come April the poplars on the road line resemble golden rockets lined up to fire. Tall, bold and brassy, they wave gently in the breeze, as if to say 'Goodbye summer, hello winter.' Then the black poplars with their white, candy-like down give the appearance of the landscape being wrapped in cotton wool. In the winter the frosts dismantle the trees so they stand naked and bare on a carpet of snow. Finally, the warmth of spring entices the catkins out in the willows until they take on a glorious chartreuse colour, like a good French liqueur.

The silver birches at Morven Hills, 1971.

Visitors

While some might think we were isolated at Morven Hills, we rarely felt that way ourselves. There were always people coming to stay, neighbours calling in, workers to feed and, later on, paying tourists to host. It was a privilege to share our high-country life with them all.

IN 1955 I RECEIVED a phone call from a stranger who introduced himself as Arthur Kitto, the part-owner of Johnson's Fish Shop in Dunedin. He told me he was an older brother of rabbiters Cyril and Vince and that he sometimes holidayed in their crib by the Morven Hills bridge. He told me he had been in touch with the Ministry of Works regarding four workmen's huts situated by the river on the Queen's chain, and wanted our permission to cross the land to get to the huts, which were leftovers from the time the bridge had been built.

The result was that the Kittos have holidayed there for almost 60 years; rearranging the cabins, cleaning and scrubbing to make them homely and habitable, and finally giving them a lovely spruce-coloured coat of paint. They mainly came at Easter and Christmas with their two children, Geoff and Glennis. Arthur was very generous and always came with a lovely parcel of fish, and we formed a close and warm friendship with him and his first wife Rose.

In later years Rose spent increasing amounts of time in the Lindis. She was kind and generous and we all loved her. She got on well with the boys and often in the summer holidays she and Peter would try their hand gold-panning at the Blue Slip corner. I don't think they ever got a speck but it filled in many afternoons. Around this time the boys had a kayak. They would put it in at the same Blue Slip corner and manoeuvre it down to the Kitto cottage. Rose was such a good sport; she would go out with them even though she'd always be tipped into the river. There was so much hilarity, I suspect she would have been disappointed if she had remained dry. The river was so low that at times they had to pick the kayak up and carry it. They were all blissfully happy, laughing and playing together.

When Rose was there she'd come up for an evening meal at least once a week. Occasionally she would pop up in the afternoons as well, get out the griddle that I kept in the back porch and make a batch of pikelets for afternoon tea.

At a barbecue over the festive season one year, I let it slip that I'd paid a deposit to go on a trek to Nepal. Rose immediately wanted to know who was going to look after the boys. I told her I was going to advertise for a housekeeper. 'Don't,' she said, 'I'll come.' And she did. It was a lovely feeling to leave and know they were all cared for.

When I returned from the trip I found the family unit in great shape. Rose had done a fantastic job looking after the folks and welcomed me home with a roast dinner. She'd even entertained a Japanese couple who arrived unexpectedly. She told me she gave the men fried eggs and homemade chips every lunchtime and then cooked meat at night. We paid her housekeeper's wages and off she drove to Dunedin as happy as a skylark.

We were lucky to have that time. At the beginning of the following May we had a very sad letter from Rose. A scan had shown that she had cancer which had spread to her glands and other parts. We felt sick with sadness. How do you write to someone who is dying? Rose had been an intrinsic part of our lives at Morven Hills. I said we would miss her company, the delicious vanilla slice which she always made for Max and the pikelets which she whipped up at the drop of her hat. We would miss the summer barbecues, the way she scattered the lupin seed which she collected every summer, meeting her grandchildren when they came to the Lindis to visit and her canoeing down the river. Rose was a bit of a dark horse about her age, and no one knew for sure how old she was. It wasn't a great surprise when her daughter Glennis rang to say her mother had passed away in her sleep on 29 April 1984.

We also made firm friends with the Robson family of Oamaru, who took us up on the offer of renting the cookhouse after the shearing had finished in January. After the new cookhouse was built in 1961 I'd had the idea of advertising it as a holiday cottage in the 'holiday accommodation' column in the *Otago Daily Times*. After all, we had a tennis court, a river just over the bank and horses to ride. The tariff would be £2 a day. When Dave Robson, a stock agent with the North Otago Farmers' Co-op, rang to see if we'd have room for their three daughters, Max said, 'You can bring all fourteen if you like,' because that was the number of beds we had. Dave, his wife Ella and their daughters Beverley, Kay and Heather holidayed with us for the next four consecutive years, usually for three weeks each time.

IN THE 1950s the road through the Lindis was unsealed and very rough, with enormous pot-holes and plenty of dust. The traffic was very light and the only thing you could depend on was that the Mt Cook bus would pass the gate twice a day. Imagine my surprise when I was raking up autumn leaves one day and suddenly heard the click of the gate. When I looked up I saw a gaunt, emaciated man ambling towards me. He was short in stature with a wrinkled face not unlike a dried prune, and was carrying a sugar bag over his shoulder. 'Gotcha some onions,' he said, tipping them out on the grass. When I asked him where he'd come from he told me that he was living in the concrete hut down by the old boarding-house in the gorge. He was trying to eke out a living by mining gold.

'Oh,' I said. 'You're Mr Thompson?'

'Nope, I'm Wattie.'

Great was my surprise to see him because stories abounded as to his dislike of the female species. 'I'll make you a cup of tea.'

'Nope,' he said, 'I don't drink tea.'

'Well, let me give you some meat.'

'Nope, don't eat meat.'

'Well, I'll drive you home.'

'Nope, I came up by the river and walking's good for yer.'

It was about this time that Wattie must have had a sudden rush of blood to the head, and walked from one end of New Zealand to the other, carrying a sandwich board which read: 'REPENT: JESUS WILL SAVE YOU.' Word got out that he had saved enough money for a flight to Antarctica, but it was cloudy and overcast and he didn't see much, so he cashed in more gold and booked himself on another. Wattie was on the ill-fated Erebus flight on 28 November 1979.

A BOOK WHICH GREATLY appealed to me was *To Sir With Love* by the West Indian author E.R. Braithwaite. I'm a slow reader and each night I would read another chapter. 'What an amazing man,' I would mutter when the lights went out.

It was December, we were shearing, Max was working long days and he'd had enough; he sat bolt upright in bed and with a loud expletive said, 'I'm tired of hearing about that man! Write and tell him what you think, but don't mention it again to me.' End of conversation!

As was my usual habit, I spent Sunday afternoon writing letters. I typed a letter to my mother and another to Max's mother, as I did every week. Max's comment filtered through my brain and I thought, why not? I found a blue aerogramme and hand-wrote a very unpretentious letter to E.R. Braithwaite, saying how I was enjoying his book and wishing him well for the future. I showed it to Max (he said 'Good'), addressed it care of the publishers and put it in the mail. Imagine our surprise when, four months later, I received a reply from Paris! Mr Braithwaite said books were an author's bread and butter, but letters of appreciation were the strawberries and cream. I didn't reply to that — I had made my point and that was the end.

There was another surprise early in 1963 when we received a letter from Mr Braithwaite, posted in Paris, in which he said 'events had conspired to his advantage'. He was being sponsored by UNESCO to undertake a lecture tour of Australasia. He also said he was working in Paris as an educational consultant and lecturer and it was his wish that he could meet people who had written to him. There was a brief itinerary of South Island places. So, at the end of May we left Karitane nurse Eleanor Shaw to look after the children while Mother took over the cooking and we drove down to Dunedin. When we got to the airport Mr Braithwaite (now known to us as E.R.B.) was easy to spot as there weren't many West Indians in Dunedin at the time! He was genuinely pleased to see us and suggested we have a drink together after the lecture. By the time we'd spent a very pleasant hour at the City Hotel we were on Christian-name terms; he said to call him Rick.

E.R.B. was so interested in our life that we said it was a pity his stay in Dunedin was such a short one, otherwise he could have come and stayed. He said that life was full of surprises.

Well, in November 1969, we received a letter from E.R.B. from New York to say he was coming to spend a week with us on the farm! No dates were given, but within weeks we received a call from him in Christchurch to say he had arrived and was chartering a plane and flying down to Luggate.

If anyone asked us which month was the best time to visit, we always nominated November because that's when all the action was. Every day the men went out on the hill and brought more sheep in, which meant there was constant activity in the yards. Just watching the dogs working enthralled most people and of course at shearing time there was a constant hum of noise as six men peeled the wool off the sheep's backs and continual action in the shed.

E.R.B. never asked when the best time was to come, but he'd hit the jackpot. Once we'd sorted out his meals, that was. I discovered he was almost a vegetarian, never ate red meat and mainly lived on fish. Thankfully, he loved omelettes. He rose early, had a couple of mornings out on a muster and was genuinely intrigued with country life. He enjoyed watching all the goings-on, and the day-to-day running of a sheep farm. And what's more, he played a sparkling game of tennis. He was utterly charming.

After lunch one day I was cleaning up in the sink while he was sitting at the kitchen table. I had the dish-mop handle in my hand, and with the fluffy bit held to my mouth, like an imaginary microphone, I went round to where he was sitting. I said, 'I'd like to interview you for the N.Z. Broadcasting Corporation.' He replied, 'Yes ma'am, go ahead.' For the first 10 minutes we were quite sensible and it was all very enlightening but then I got the giggles and he began to laugh too. 'Mr Braithwaite,' I said, 'having read several of your books, I think you have a chip on your shoulder.' 'Oh no,' he said, 'I have a chip on each shoulder. It gives me a more balanced outlook.' Then we both collapsed into giggles. It was so much fun. I wished we had a real tape.

When we took him to Christchurch airport to catch his plane to Los Angeles he neglected to write his ethnic origin on his departure card. 'Excuse me,' said the overbearing little

Max and me with E.R. Braithwaite,
Milford Sound, 2005.

man who sat behind the counter, as he looked directly at Mr Braithwaite. 'What race?'

'Put me down for the hurdles,' said E.R.B., as quick as a flash.

I saw E.R.B. again when we visited him in Washington in 2005. On the bus one day, E.R.B. told me he would love to come back to New Zealand for one more trip. The news stunned me because I knew he was in his nineties, but I said we would meet him in Queenstown any time. In the middle of October 2005, he flew out and spent 16 days with us. We did all the touristy things, landing on the glacier at Mt Cook, a night at the Glenorchy Hotel, a jet-boat ride up the Dart River, a flight and landing at Milford Sound, followed by coffee at the hotel, and Richard took him up in the farm helicopter and over Lake Wanaka. For his age, he was quite remarkable: no glasses, no hearing aids, no walking stick. He hardly ever writes now but he rang me on 27 June 2012 and told me he was celebrating his hundredth birthday. Such an extraordinary man.

IN OUR EARLY YEARS at Morven Hills, I had the bright idea of having overseas paying guests to stay. Max wasn't so keen; he said, 'We're a farming operation and not a tourist attraction.' I countered by saying we had young children and couldn't travel, so why not have the world come to us? We were on the tourist route, halfway between Queenstown and Mt Cook, and if visitors didn't have a car, they could come by bus. It was a golden opportunity. We tossed the idea around and after a few days Max agreed we could give it a go. I wrote a letter to the Government Tourist Bureau in Auckland explaining we lived in the high country, on the tourist route, and were keen to host overseas guests. They didn't reply so I wrote a similar letter and sent it off to the Government Tourist Bureau in Wellington. They didn't reply either so, third time lucky, off went another letter to the Government

Tourist Bureau in Christchurch. Still no reply, and I thought if that's all they care, they can stuff it up their jumper; I won't bother with Dunedin.

On the afternoon of 19 January 1966, the children were playing outside when they suddenly came running in to get me. 'Mum, there's a big black car coming up the drive!' When the car drew up the man who got out introduced himself as Ron Silcock, the manager of the Government Tourist Bureau in Dunedin. He told me that all three letters had been forwarded to him and he was making an assessment call. I'm sure he came unannounced so he could see what kind of a housekeeper I was.

After I showed him through the house, we had fresh scones for afternoon tea and discussed the situation. I told him how the idea had evolved and that the guests would have to take us as they found us. Max was a working farmer, so if he came in wearing dirty clothes, that's because he was doing a dirty job. There'd be no pretention and no dressing up. I told him our winters were very cold and unpleasant and that we'd prefer not to have anyone between May and September. I stipulated I wouldn't have anyone for more than a week, and please, only English-speaking overseas guests. No New Zealanders. No children.

Mr Silcock listened, wrote everything down and nodded in agreement. We discussed tariffs and he suggested £4 per person a day. That seemed an enormous amount so I was happy and we settled on that. Three months later, on 28 March 1966, we had our first guest, an English lady, Mrs Rachel Davenport, who came for a week. From there on in, and for the next 20 years, we were in business. We had loads of interesting people from all walks of life: doctors, dentists, accountants, pilots, undertakers (well — one), travel agents and veterinarians but, rather surprisingly, no farmers. The homestays took off so well that guests started to return for second and third visits.

We always had breakfast and lunch in the kitchen and then set up dinner in the dining room. In the evenings we always had pre-dinner drinks and on the odd occasion a bottle of wine with our meal. During the day, if the men were coming

top
Max collecting water for a picnic.

bottom
Max at the cattleyards.

in for morning or afternoon smoko, the guests would join them. The secret was to have everything homemade — the jam, preserved fruit, soup, muesli and most other things were made by me. The meat came off the farm, as did most of the vegetables. The small fruits of summer grew in great abundance so we'd have weeks of fresh blackcurrants, strawberries and raspberries. One American man went into raptures when he saw the rhubarb growing. He lived in a high-rise apartment in Manhattan and said the rhubarb reminded him of his childhood in Wisconsin; 'You can give me rhubarb three times a day, I just love it,' he said. So I did. I even tried my hand at rhubarb muffins and he loved them too. When he went to stay at the Hermitage at Mt Cook I gave him six in a bag to take with him. He had a chauffeur with him and when the driver went round to pick up his cases he said, very loudly, 'Forget the luggage, but be sure to pick up the muffins!'

Max was marvellous and, weather permitting, he always planned his work so he could take visitors out in the four-wheel-drive vehicle to one of the back huts. On occasion they'd stop there for a pre-packed picnic lunch. Our country rose a mile high and on a clear day the views were out of this world, stretching out to Mt Aspiring and Mt Cook.

Hosting bachelors was a lot of work. They frequently arrived with a suitcase of dirty washing and numerous shirts. Luckily I didn't mind ironing. After all, 'Keep the guests happy' was my motto. The worst part was that they always asked the same mundane questions: 'How many acres?', 'How many sheep?', 'How many dogs?', 'How do you train them?', 'How many children?' and so on. I wondered if I should write the answers down on a big blackboard and place it in their room. Then I had an idea; I said to them, 'Now, you're only allowed ten questions.'

My other major problem was that when guests left they always asked that we keep in touch. It was impossible. I spent hours pondering if I needed a chef in the kitchen or a secretary in the office. Although I wrote a long newsy Christmas letter for several years, the lists grew ever longer and the postage greater, so I eventually gave it up. But I've kept a record of every single person who passed through our home. With the advent of email I've been able to stay in touch with several, but, alas, with the passing of time, most of them are now in their nineties.

ONE OF OUR EARLY GUESTS, Eric Tucker from Surrey, England, first came and stayed in 1972. Eric had worked for British Airways all his life and every year he was given a round-the-world first-class air ticket. As a bachelor with no ties he was free to avail himself of this magnificent bonus.

Eric was an enigma. He was fascinating, charming, considerate, a tremendous shopper, a wonderful host and very good in the house. He loved helping me, but had little passion for the outdoors. Rarely did he participate in the farming activities in which, to be honest, most guests loved to be included. To begin with he always came for a week but he fitted into the family so well that his visits increased week by week, year after year. During his last few visits he would come for three months at a time, the entire summer. In all he had 14 consecutive visits, and occasionally he'd pop an extra visit in during the year. We were all genuinely fond of him and before long he started to feel like one of the family. I have no doubt he looked on us as family.

He'd arrive on the Mt Cook bus from Christchurch. When the bus stopped at the Forest Range gate (opposite Morven Hills) family members and assorted pets would always be waiting to meet him. Often I'd put him in a side bedroom, and we continued with our regular homestays using the en suite. We called him Eric Snow, our English butler.

Eric came with us when we walked the Routeburn Track in January 1976. He flew out at the end of November as usual and then spent December with Max's rucksack on his back, filled with 18 pounds (about 8 kilograms) of rocks. I know it was 18 pounds because he made the boys check it on the wool scales in the woolshed. He wasn't fit but did his best to counteract this. Rain or sunshine he walked up to the fertiliser bins at the top of the airstrip, rucksack on his back, and staggered back to the house with a face resembling a good claret. We did the Routeburn with an organised group and began at the Milford end. It was a wonderful trip.

We often met up with Eric on our trips to England and often stayed with him in London. He would always take me into the china department at the Allders store in Croydon and I had a field day. Some people buy shoes or clothes but I didn't buy either of those — my pet weakness (after plants) was china. I bought, at different times, three sets of the blue-and-white 36-piece 'Yorktown' set by Royal Doulton, which gave me a 108-piece dinner set. Later, I bought an eight-piece Italian Spode set, complete with coffee cups and saucers. If Max was with me we'd bring a set home, otherwise I'd leave them for Eric to bring out as he always had a business-class ticket but very little personal luggage. When he arrived at Customs in Auckland he always told them it was for his bach in the Lindis (i.e. the shearers' quarters!). I could never have done it without his help.

Eric was such a generous man. When we were building our new house in 1985, I mentioned in my weekly letter to him that we couldn't buy a collapsible ladder for the attic. He answered, 'Don't worry, I'll buy one and fly out with it,' which he did. Nothing was a bother for Eric. He did lots of shopping for other people as well. In later years when Peter needed a housekeeper while recuperating after his accident, Eric flew out especially and looked after him magnificently.

In March 1990 the phone rang with a late-night call. It was Eric, calling from England. He said, 'I've got Pickfords here and I'm packing up my dinner set to send you.' I was so shocked that I asked him if he had been on the cooking sherry. 'No, no,' he replied, 'you are like family to me and I want you to have it. I know you like blue-and-white china and I'm sorry this is green, but it is my wish that someone in the Snow family will use it.'

Three months later we drove up to Lyttelton with the

trailer, filled in numerous forms, cleared Customs and came straight home with the bounty. Eric, being Eric, had sent me an itemised list of all the contents and we did as we were told, and ticked everything off. It was a bit like being bequeathed the contents of an Aladdin's cave. The three packing cases contained a 12-piece Spode Byron dinner set, with a note from Spode to say the pattern had been withdrawn in 1963. In addition there were soup plates, a soup tureen with lid and ladle, numerous round vegetable dishes with lids, assorted shapes without lids, six large oval meat platters, three coffee pots, teapots, three assorted jugs, a mint-sauce boat and gravy boat, sugar bowl, egg cups, coffee cups and saucers, fruit bowls, a covered cheese dish, pepper and salt shakers, a mustard pot, 14 crescent salad plates, a muffin dish, two marmalade jars with lids and 15 teacups and saucers. There were well over 100 pieces, all in the same Spode pattern and not one thing broken. A man came to the house as we were unpacking and said, 'I'll give you ten thousand dollars for the lot, as is,' but we weren't interested.

In due course, with a lot of rearranging, we managed to pack it away in the cupboards. When I was younger I would use it at least three times a year for smart dinner parties and then I would ring Eric and say, 'Mr Spode is out tonight.' There was always a one-word reply: 'Marvellous.'

GUESTS WERE OFTEN very generous. I had recipe books sent to me from all over the world (it made me wonder if there was something amiss with my cooking) and pictorial journals from many American states. Eric kept sending me pieces of Royal Albert china which were gift wrapped and beautifully packaged, and always arrived in mint condition.

I loved the mail. It was a link with the outside world. I love the feel and smell of letters, and a handwritten one is much more personal than the emails of today. Although he typed

top
Eric Tucker shelling peas with Annabelle and a pup.

bottom
Eric became a regular visitor and was always given a big welcome on his arrival.

his, Eric was an inveterate letter writer. When he went home to England I could count on getting two a week from him. In all the years I knew him, he never used the word 'love'. All his letters ended 'bye' and that was it.

By 1973 we'd been having guests for seven years and the daily tariff had increased to $12 per person. Although this seemed a lot to me, it didn't discourage people from coming. It was immensely stimulating to have new people week after week. All three children were at school in Christchurch by this stage, but farming and tourism continued at the same fast pace. Wool was bringing a good price and although many a swimming pool made an appearance in farmers' gardens at this time, we were perfectly happy with the Lindis River over the bank. I truly loved my life.

I was getting lots of bookings from the Government Tourist Bureau in Auckland and Christchurch when we received a surprise letter from the head office of Newmans Coach Lines. The Ministry of Works was about to start about six weeks of work realigning the Nevis Bluff. During this time the road would be open for a short period in the morning and then closed until midday. As their tour buses would need to leave earlier than usual, would we be able to provide lunch for the tour parties? I rang Doreen Still and asked if she would be prepared to help. I said I would pay her $5 an hour. That sounds like slave labour now, but at the time, the minimum hourly wage was $2.30. Then I rang the butcher in Cromwell and asked if he would meet the Mt Cook bus and send me sliced ham on the days I ordered it. Once we were all in agreement I got in touch with Newmans and gave them the green light. They estimated that there would be one, maybe two tours a week. Most days there would be 25 passengers, nearly all from overseas, and they would pay me $2 a head.

I drove through to Timaru, had a night with Mother and bought enough china and cutlery and dishes to cater for 40 people. Blue is my favourite colour so naturally everything was blue. I then got the builders to make me two long trestles. Then I had to work out what to feed our visitors. I listened to Alison Holst regularly on the radio and read her weekly cooking page. The message she was always trying to impart was to remember: KISS (Keep it Simple, Stupid), so I decided to do just that. Ham and salads would be followed by pavlova, usually three for a tour, with fresh fruit. I know lots of people scorn pavlova, but I consider them to be a New Zealand symbol and we had to do something with all my lovely free-range eggs.

I quickly discovered the first thing bus people look for is a toilet stop. This is very important if you want your tours to be a success. Buses came and went and we never had any problems. Doreen was great. She and Cliff had been with us for 10 years by that stage and knew how the farm operated. She could handle all the questions that were thrown at her.

Occasionally, the men would be working at the yards or shifting sheep through the house paddock. The Americans loved to see that. Everyone was happy. We were busy, but if you're organised, you can do amazing things. Then we hit a brick wall.

Several weeks into our luncheons, I received a call from Harry Chandler, the county clerk with the Vincent County Council in Clyde, and the stop sign went out. He said the council had received a formal complaint from Mary Ruffell who owned and operated the Tarras tearooms. She alleged I was trying to put her out of business. It was laughable. When I asked what I had to do to continue with the tours, Mr Chandler said I had to apply to the council for resource consent. While our lawyer said he would appear before the council, I decided I knew the facts better than anyone and would front up myself. Armed with all the relevant information, the letter from Newmans and the chits that had been signed by all the drivers, I sallied forth to Clyde, met the council, went over all the facts and then placed the documents on the table. By now the Nevis Bluff had been repaired and the buses had reverted to their old timetable. I explained that I had not set out to do luncheon tours but a series of circumstances had exposed a need which I grasped with both hands. Did they want me to showcase the high country or to sit in my La-Z-Boy chair and stick to my knitting? At the end of the month I had a letter from the council informing me I had been granted consent. I was over the moon; I could do what I liked in my own home with no penalty. With Doreen's help I continued to do luncheon tours for Newmans, and many other groups as well, until 1985. By this time they were paying $8 a head.

The early summer day of 17 November 1980 began as any normal day. We were shearing as usual, and all the men were drafting at the yards. The president of the Women's Division of Federated Farmers in Hawea had rung the week before to see if they could bring a busload over to look at the garden and the woolshed. They chartered the local school bus and arrived with their lunch around mid-morning. It was a school bus so the driver had to leave at 2 p.m. sharp in order to be back in Hawea to pick up the school children at 3 p.m. When it came time to leave, one visitor, George Nicholson Hall, was missing. When there was no sign of him anywhere we presumed he'd gone down to the river to look at the old buildings. The driver had just left when the cook came running across the paddock. 'I've found him,' she gasped, 'but he ain't going back on any bus, he's departed already.' During a detour through the pine trees, Mr Hall had had a massive heart attack and died. Had Ngaio Marsh been here I'm sure she would have produced a bestseller! She wrote a book called *Died in the Wool*, and could have followed it up with *Died in the Trees*. Never a dull moment in the Lindis.

In 1984 we had an Australian couple staying when a regular Newmans driver rang from Queenstown, asking if I would have 35 for morning tea next morning. Already busy, I said I didn't think it was possible. 'Come on, luv,' he replied, 'I know you can do it.' His powers of persuasion worked. I made two lots of shortbread that afternoon and in the morning a double batch of scones, topped them up with raspberry jam and whipped cream, and we were ready and smiling for the group of Americans. He gave me $70 cash. Bus tours were part of our lives in the seventies and eighties and we tried not to turn anyone down.

Madge's Shortbread

8 oz (220 grams) butter
2 oz (55 grams) sugar
2 oz (55 grams) icing sugar
12 oz (2 cups) plain flour
1 tablespoon cornflour
pinch of salt

Preheat the oven to 200°C.

Beat butter, sugar and icing sugar until white and fluffy. Then beat in flour, cornflour and salt. Form the mixture into two cylinders and slice off pieces. Mark the tops with an old-fashioned wooden cotton reel.

Turn the oven down to 150°C and bake for 30 minutes.

By 1984 the tariff for an overnight visitor had risen to $40 per person. At the 10-year mark it had sat at $18 a day, but we gradually increased it in the hopes it would cut back the numbers. It did a bit, but not a great deal. I told every person who passed through the house, 'Please don't tip in New Zealand, you are spoiling our country.'

THE A.A. HAD ERECTED a sign at our gate way saying 'Emergency Telephone', and you wouldn't believe how many people made use of it. There were no fuel stations between Joe Shaw at Tarras and Allan Blackie at Omarama Motors, so motorists would turn up the drive because their dashboard light had come on and they were apprehensive. At first Max would take them over to our pump and give them petrol. Sometimes they paid, but often they didn't. Max soon got sick of this, so started to keep a five-gallon container ready to sell to the next caller. He knew five gallons would get them safely over the Lindis.

Winter brought other problems, especially when there was a lot of snow or a series of hard frosts. It was a rare winter when Max didn't have to tow cars over the pass. Some winters he towed dozens over. It wasn't so bad in the daylight hours, but after dark it was always a nightmare.

During the school holidays in August 1970 the two boys and their friend David Badcock were lying in front of the fire, trying to make a house out of their Meccano set. It was the second day of rain that was so torrential you would think the farmers had ordered a month's supply in one day. Suddenly David looked up and said there was a car coming up the drive. Then Peter looked and said 'and another, and another'. It turned out the river was in flood, water was all over the road in the Lindis Gorge, the bridge had gone out on the Omarama side, and all these motorists had been caught in the middle. There were 27 of them in all!

My giddy aunt! There were old ladies, young ladies, honeymooners, farmers, wine merchants and even someone I remembered from my Craighead days: Gertrude Sykes, who was by now married to Robin Gould. They were on their way to Queenstown to celebrate the birthday of Robin and his twin brother Humphrey. We wondered what we'd do with everyone. Twenty-seven unexpected guests is quite a handful.

First, a meal. Fortunately I'd made a huge pot of soup so I just added to this. 'Huge' in the country means really enormous, so there was plenty to go around. I heated up the soup and Max, John Stokes and Bill Felton, who had been attending a farmers' meeting in Omarama, buttered mountains of toast. The wine merchant brought in bottles of wine and insisted on pouring a glass of wine. He and Max had a stand-up argument, Max saying, 'You can't bring wine into this house,' and the man saying, 'This is my wine and you can't tell me what to do with it; after all we have a birthday to celebrate.'

The honeymooners refused to sleep in the house and took themselves off to the cookhouse. There was no heating over there so they must have nearly frozen, but that was their choice. Max suddenly remembered that over in the woolshed we had a dozen brand-new mattresses, still with the plastic sheeting round them. They were to replace the nine-year-old ones in the shearers' quarters that the union lady had declared to be substandard. Max and the boys, along with John and Bill, took the Land Rover over, piled it high with all the brand-new mattresses, covered them with a tarpaulin (it was still raining) and distributed them between various rooms, turning them into dormitories. We then collected up all the blankets and rugs we could find. Then people worked out which dormitory they wanted to sleep in. We had male and female dormitories. My boys top-and-tailed in one bedroom. People were sleeping everywhere — it was reminiscent of wartime during the Blitz. It was feverish fun.

We weren't sure how long the road would be out so I took two legs of mutton out of the freezer in readiness for lunch next day. John Stokes, bless him, was first up in the morning and took everyone a cup of tea and a piece of homemade shortbread. He earned a few brownie points for that. A reporter with the *Otago Daily Times* rang, as did the police and the *Oamaru Mail*; they were all worried about the food situation. By late morning the weather was clearing, the river had dropped dramatically and the Ministry of Works was checking the road to see if traffic could get through, clearing rocks at the same time. Our guests all enjoyed their roast lunch before news came through at 2 p.m. it was all clear. The 27 tourists went on their way and the boys settled down with their Meccano set again. As I said to one newspaper, it was like a dream. A week later, I could hardly believe it had happened.

IN 1964 I BOUGHT my first Douglas Badcock painting. Douglas and Bonnie Badcock were living on Frankton Road, Queenstown and I drove over specifically to buy a painting to mask our bare walls. My first choice was the poplar grove at Whitechapel, Arrowtown. It was very reminiscent of the poplars at Morven Hills and I knew I would never tire of looking at it. After Bonnie invited me in for afternoon tea we chatted away and Douglas asked if he could come to Morven Hills and paint some of the old buildings. That day marked the beginning of my long love affair with Badcock paintings.

From then on the Badcocks were regular visitors. They'd come with their caravan and take it down the track to the flat grassy area down by the river. It was a quiet, private and very sheltered place. Doug would spend every day outside, furiously painting the old buildings — he did a splendid one of Polson's hut. Doug and Bonnie's son David, who at nine or 10 was in between Richard and Peter, loved the farm so much that from then on he spent most of his school holidays at Morven Hills. They all got on famously, and you have to throw Geoff Still, son of Cliff and Doreen, into the mix. Even at that early age you could see David had enormous talent and that he'd go a long way in the art world.

Bonnie Badcock became one of my best friends. A softly spoken, gentle lady, Bonnie was the glue that held the family together while art and painting consumed Doug's entire life. It was an enormous privilege and thrill to be a friend of Doug's. Often he would say he was going painting up the Ahuriri Valley, to the Clay Cliffs at Omarama or down by the old boarding house in the Lindis. 'Would you like to come with us?' No matter what I was doing, I'd drop everything and go. I never once turned down the invitation.

To see Doug in action was unbelievable. A dozen dabs of the brush and you could see the outline of the subject. Talent and energy appeared to flow down his arm. Bonnie would clean Doug's brushes so he could just keep on painting — it was usual for him to finish each painting in two hours. It was such pure magic that I never tired of watching. When we were around the old buildings, Doug would finish a painting in less time than it took me to whip up a batch of scones.

In 1980 Doug rang during shearing. He and Bonnie were coming over with their caravan and he wanted to paint the shearers in action. Although he had previously done several of the inside of the shed, none of them had come to life once he put the shearers in. Over the next four days Doug did a basic outline of the inside and then painted the shearers in. They didn't look right so he turned the board over and went through the same routine. He wanted to be able to look at the painting and feel the 'action'. It wasn't happening, but he kept trying. Eventually the presser stopped by and said, 'Looks like you're having a bad week,' but Doug laughed and stuck to his guns.

He was still trying by day four. Just before dinner Doug appeared at the house, doubled up with laughter, with floods of tears running down his face. He was so choked up, he could hardly speak. He said in his 60 years he had heard his paintings called all kinds of things but never an 'arsehole'! It turned out the Aussie presser had assumed that he was churning out the paintings for sale and said, 'Blimey, they'll

Douglas Badcock painting the old Lindis Hotel (top)
and the shearing shed at Morven Hills (bottom).

be like an arsehole, everyone will have one.'

Eventually Doug did execute a beauty, depicting the board with all six shearers. Max was so impressed that he offered $10,000 for it, but Doug turned it down. Perhaps it was a commission. I would love to know what happened to it. Incidentally, Max's favourite painting in the house was one of the inside of the woolshed, minus shearers, that Doug painted in 1977.

Doug Badcock wasn't the only artist who visited Morven Hills; every spring artists flocked to the old buildings like bees to the apple blossom. In 1980, Gisborne artist Peter Brown came and painted the old stables that Jock McLean had built. It was such a beauty that I offered to buy it on the spot. I paid $250 for it, unframed.

During the 1975 August school holidays the boys spent most of their time catching turkeys which they sold for pocket money. I can't say I was choked up with delight about it. After they'd plucked a dozen or so birds their hair and clothes were covered with feathers and the smell was indescribable. Still, it's what boys do. One afternoon Richard came in and said they'd been chasing turkeys down at the old cookhouse across the river and had come across a nice man doing a painting of the building. Richard added, 'He's got gold in the front of his teeth and he's wearing green socks, and I've asked him up for a cup of tea.' Shortly afterwards we got to meet Ken Andrews, and later on, his lovely wife, Irma. Ken had been chief subeditor of the *Timaru Herald*, but in 1974 he resigned so he could paint. Irma had a baby-clothes shop in the Timaru Arcade and did the most wonderful smocking.

Although Ken loved painting the old buildings, he was also a dab hand on alpine flowers, both in watercolours and in oils. I commissioned him to do colour paintings of the three different gentians that grew in my Lindis garden: *Gentiana sino ornata*, *Gentiana acaulis* and *Gentiana verna*. I have all three paintings hanging in the kitchen.

After Ken died in 1987, I had Irma to stay each year. She was never idle. She would always be smocking a gown for a new baby, knitting a jersey or a pair of socks for the grandchildren, or making a sewing box for a friend. I always made several batches of Belgian biscuits when Irma came; she'd sit and join them together with raspberry jam, and then ice them. Once when we were working together she said, 'It takes face powder to get a man, but baking powder to keep him.'

BEFORE CHRISTMAS 1984 the Mt Cook Company rang to see if we would host a journalist from Auckland for four days as they wanted to publish an article on a sheep station in their *Inflight* magazine. So on 16 January 1985, Julia Thorne flew to Queenstown, picked up a rental car and drove over. Peter was watching cricket and I was in the shower when she arrived. Mother had rung to see if I had dusted the house as she knew housework wasn't one of my strong points, but I told her Julia wasn't about to write about dust (I always tell folk it helps keep the furniture warm). Julia fitted in with whatever the men were doing and she had a very pleasant personality. It was like having a cousin to stay.

I thought the article was splendid. Truthful writing, nothing flowery, and her photography was top notch too. It was called 'Home on the Range'. Here are a few excerpts:

> A tall, dark, lean young man greets me at the door — Peter — No. 2 son — and shows me to the guest room — fresh, with Sanderson-print bedding in blues and cream, a bathroom en suite. 'Mum will be out shortly,' Peter explains as we watch progress in the one-day Pakistan v New Zealand test match on television. My radio faded out on the drive from Queenstown and I still can't actually see the ball — it is one of the fuzzy dots. 'We only get half a channel up here,' Peter explains, 'pay the full licence fee of course, but only half a channel.'

Madge breezes through to the living room with a welcome. Visitors are a regular item — even way out here. For 20 years the family has hosted overseas guests directed to Morven Hills by the Government Tourist Bureau.

Madge doesn't participate in the farm work — but must be one of the most professional 'farmer's wives' around. She has never bought a jar of jam in her life. Pickles, sauces, everything through to honey in the comb is homemade — except the Vegemite. Biscuit tins are constantly full . . . Max's vegetable garden produces enough potatoes to last the whole year: beetroot, corn, carrots, lettuce, cabbages, swedes, peas, tomatoes — you name it and Madge more than likely has it fresh, frozen and preserved.

Max, not at all the rough-and-ready high-country shepherd one might expect, joins us in the evening ritual of a G & T before dinner. It is easy to see where Peter's traits originate. Both look limber, Max, a 58-year-old, fit, with a deep outdoor tan, and both hold an air of responsibility.

Dinners are a grand affair and this is no exception — family silver, wine and a sumptuous meal . . . there is a hot roast leg of lamb, fresh garden vegetables and home-grown raspberries in the offering. 'The men don't feel as though they've eaten really, unless we have a pudding of some sort,' Madge says.

top
A painting by Douglas Badcock.

bottom
Richard and Max in the woolshed.

Air Force adventures

In April 1970, artist Colin Wheeler and his wife Phyllis came from Oamaru for a week, ostensibly to work on a book on high-country sheep stations.

FIFTY-ONE AT THE TIME, Colin had previously worked as art teacher at the Waitaki Boys' High School in Oamaru. Colin's first book had sold well and publishers A.H. & A.W. Reed were keen for him to follow it up with book number two. Colin was a quiet and modest man, small in stature and gentle in demeanour, but there was nothing mousey about him. He would stand with a large pad in one hand, pencil in the other, and just draw. No rubbing out, no mistakes, first time perfect. I would stand behind him and gape as he drew all the old buildings, the woolshed (inside and out), the cookhouse, stables and even the dog kennels. Phyllis accompanied him everywhere and gave him advice as to what should go in the book. We enjoyed their company and discussed everything under the sun.

Near the end of his stint it was suggested Colin should draw the old miner's hut on the top side of the road at the entrance to the pass, beyond the Blue Slip. It had a hexagonal chimney and was built so perfectly that it was always a good talking point. It may even have been built by the same men who built the woolshed. Max drove him out there in the Land Rover. Colin was sketching away in mid-afternoon when a plane flew low between the hills — the Royal New Zealand Air Force were conducting a low-flying exercise out of Queenstown and every day there were planes flying up and down our valley. 'My God,' said Colin, 'I hope he knows what he is doing. He is far too low for comfort.'

The next morning we were having our breakfast in the kitchen when I told the assembled company about the dream I had had. I never remember my dreams and that's why it was so remarkable. In my dream a plane flying up the valley had got into trouble and crashed into the side of the hill. Colin said that was bizarre because he'd been dreaming of helicopters landing and taking off near the woolshed. He asked, had we eaten too much cheese? After he and Phyllis had finished their porridge and drunk their tea, Colin walked over to the wall, picked up his easel and sketching pad, then wheeled round and patted me on the back, with a 'Looks like you and I are both up in the air today' comment. 'Happy landings,' he said as they went out the door.

The phone rang. It was Jeanette Emerson, who with Russell had taken over Forest Range from his grandparents, George and Elsie Henderson. They were inviting us and the Wheelers for dinner that night. After dinner we were chatting away when, some time after 9 p.m., Russell said, 'Shh, is that the phone ringing?' When all had quietened down, we heard our ring on the party line so Russell suggested Max answer it there and then. We heard him say, 'Yes, I do live in the Lindis Pass.' It was the Air Search and Rescue in Wellington explaining that one of the Air Force's Devons was missing in the Lindis. An Air Force Orion had been dispatched from Auckland and was picking up a signal from the downed aircraft somewhere in the Lindis. They asked if we would go to a clear area, and at exactly 11 p.m. the Orion would drop three flares directly over the spot the signal was coming from. Then Max was to ring them back in Wellington and help them pinpoint the area.

We drove up to the airstrip with the Wheelers. In the still of the night it was eerily quiet and pitch black. On the hill you could hear the occasional bleating of sheep and, away in the distance, the gentle throb of an aircraft, gradually getting closer and louder. As we all piled out of the car we could discern the red blinking light of the Orion. When, at exactly 11 p.m., they dropped three flares, it was like seeing falling stars. Max pinpointed the area as being on Eric Goodger's Breast Hill property and rang the Air Search headquarters in Wellington.

For the next two weeks Morven Hills was like Piccadilly Circus. The next morning Max and I jumped out of bed at 5 a.m. Less than half an hour later the Air Search and Rescue crew were showing Max maps of the area and asking him to indicate where the crash could be. Three men who had driven through the night from Timaru were needing breakfast. By 7 a.m., 22 men had converged from all points of the compass. Tom Lloyd, a photographer representing the *Otago Daily Times*, was one of the first on the scene. We fed them tinned spaghetti with poached eggs on toast. I then made a big batch of scones in readiness for the next group and Phyllis whipped up a bowl of cream. Colin counted 30 men for morning tea. Trays of scones were coming out of the oven in factory-like quantities. Unknown men, mainly journalists and reporters, were wafting through the kitchen, snatching cups of tea and hot scones and chain-smoking as they tried to prise out as much information as possible.

Then the big guns began to arrive. Fred Kinvig, Ron Chippindale, John Harris and Jim McKnight, all members of the Air Force Court of Enquiry, arrived by Iroquois. We coped with 30 for lunch by feeding two relays of 15 people. I made a big pot of mince, Phyllis buttered toast to go under and Colin was in charge of cups of tea. As I prepared more food, Phyllis and Colin washed and dried dishes. I couldn't have managed without them.

By 7.30 a.m. the Search and Rescue planners had worked out a strategy and the rescue team drove to the Blue Slip corner, left their vehicles there and then walked inland. After two and a half hours of uphill slog the wreckage was found in a steep, cul-de-sac gully. When it was discovered that three men had died, the Air Force swung into action, taking over our cookshop and making Morven Hills their operational base. Every day, Iroquois helicopters landed and took off directly opposite the kitchen window, their deep 'thud thud' stabbing our peaceful little valley.

The Air Force personnel walked to the scene and back each day. I felt sorry for them as, come evening, they returned exhausted and then had to cook their own meal. I suggested that if they brought their provisions over to the homestead, I would have dinner ready each night. The Air Force certainly didn't stint themselves. I had to smile when the first carton unloaded from the Iroquois was a pallet of beer. Steaks the size of bathmats arrived along with enough vegetables to stock a country greengrocer, dozens of trays of eggs and sponges of squash-court proportions. During the next two weeks I made plain trifle, jelly trifle, Norwegian trifle, tiramisu and lamingtons. Despite the wretchedness and sadness of the occasion, there was friendship and camaraderie.

Towards the end of their stay Max and I had to go to Alexandra to see our accountant, so I told the men that they would have to get their own dinner. Next evening they volunteered the information that they had used up 70 eggs, or 'cackle berries' as one man called them. It was so incredible that I made them write down their menu on the calendar in the mini bar:

Thursday, 16 April 1970

Scrambled for breakfast	32
Lunch, steak and eggs	14
Dinner, scrambled	24
Total eggs	70

Signed B.R. Emirali, *chef*

EVENTUALLY, THEIR WORK ALL accomplished, the Air Force packed up and left. Life at Morven Hills returned to a semblance of normality.

At the time of the crash, pilot Robin Klitscher was captain of an Air Force Iroquois helicopter that was providing support to an army exercise at Lake Brunner on the West Coast. Once the news of the crash came on 7 April 1970, Robin, his helicopter and crew (co-pilot Ross Masters and Corporal Bruce Knight) were pulled out of the army exercise and dispatched to Morven Hills. Robin recalled the sad event:

> The Devon was flying up a valley and simply didn't make it. I wouldn't want to judge what happened but my understanding is that the aircraft got into a position it couldn't get out of.
>
> The flying conditions were clear, but the wind was a problem. It was very turbulent from the northwest and very unpleasant flying. The aircraft had gone down in a very narrow gully so we had to approach very, very carefully. I was able to see the debris from the crash from the pilot's seat. The wreckage was spread over a considerable area and it was quite obvious that nobody had survived. We touched down, one skid on the side of the mountain, a bit further down the slope. I remember sitting in the aircraft, holding it against the side of the hill in very blustery conditions. The crewman, Corporal Knight, put the bodies on the aircraft stretchers and we brought them out and then flew them back to Wigram.
>
> We spent several days flying members of the Court of Enquiry into the site so that they could do their investigation. It was rough country and a difficult slog on foot for the Court of Enquiry to

get up to the site. They'd be pretty exhausted by the time we picked them up and took them back to the station at the end of the day.

We camped in the Morven Hills shearers' quarters rather than flying back and forth from Queenstown every day. I remember that we were very comfortable, and that everyone was very jovial and welcoming . . . we'd come from an army exercise in the jungle in the West Coast, with tents and very basic provisions, so the contrast was quite marked! We had four full-on days before we finally left Morven Hills to go back to the West Coast on 11 April.

Morven Hills homestead and woolshed.

LATER YEARS

Taking to the skies

In the early eighties both boys started learning to fly. Richard was driving to Christchurch and having helicopter-flying lessons from Simon Spencer-Bower. Peter was also learning to fly a fixed-wing aircraft — he went to Wanaka for his lessons. By the beginning of 1985 both of them had their licences.

AT THE 1985 WANAKA A&P show, Skysales Aviation of Christchurch were demonstrating Robinson 22 helicopters. When the men arrived home they seemed convinced that it would be just the thing for Morven Hills. Even Max was smitten with the idea. They'd asked the pilot to drop in on Sunday on his way back to Christchurch so, just before 10 a.m., there was an unmistakable 'whop, whop, whop' sound coming up the valley. He flew low over the woolshed and by the time he landed right by the back gate, my three men were there to meet him.

Richard came running down the concrete path and into the kitchen, asking, 'What do you think of it, Mum?' Rather facetiously I said, 'Oh, it would be lovely if was blue and white.' The pilot/salesman, Ron Connel, who was one step behind Richard, said, 'We can paint it any colour you like.' They did, and we became the proud owners of a blue-and-white Robinson 22. We didn't have a hangar in those days, but it slid snugly into the carport. When Simon Spencer-Bower came and gave Richard a few more lessons in the hills, he told us that flying in the Lindis conditions was totally different from the flat Canterbury Plains. At morning tea he explained that most accidents were caused by pilot error and said to never take it up in fog.

In March I had my first ride in the helicopter. It was a perfect day without a breath of wind, nor a cloud in the sky, good old reliable March weather. When the boys came in for morning tea, Richard said, 'I'll get Bluebird out and take you for a flight.' 'Where to?' I asked. He suggested that if we flew down to Tarras I could do my grocery shopping in the store. I put my red jacket on and away we went. I remember thinking it was a funny feeling, as though we were suspended in space. We landed in Peter Jolly's paddock opposite the store and school, and I walked over and bought my groceries. Three months previously the school had asked if Richard would pick up 'Father Christmas' and drop him off at the school break up which was being held down by the river at Bendigo. The children were ecstatic to see the helicopter again and rushed over to the fenceline in their lunch break. When they saw an old lady with white hair and a red jacket arrive, they sang out, 'Here's Mother Christmas!' It was a shame to disillusion them, but it was a bit of a laugh. I loved the flight. It took 10 minutes each way.

In 2005 Richard detected a cairn on a high peak on Morven Hills so he landed the chopper for a closer inspection. When you think of the large number of musterers who had had a hand in bringing the sheep in over that time I find it totally

top
A cairn Richard found on one of the hills in 2005, presumably connected to the Polson family.

bottom
Richard and our first Robinson 22.

amazing that there had never been a mention of the cairn. All the men must have sent their dogs to clear the land without actually walking up. The cairn has a commanding view over Morven Hills and down the Lindis Valley.

Perhaps it was built in memory of the Polson twins who died in 1869 and were then forgotten for the next 130 years. The Polson story is a sad one. When cooper John Polson lived in Wick in the north of Scotland his main occupation was making barrels for salted herrings, which was hardly the traditional training for a high-country shepherd. However, the important thing was a willingness to give anything a go. Shortly after John arrived at Port Chalmers in 1862 he came across a flock of sheep that had just been unloaded. Despite knowing little about sheep, and even less about the Otago countryside, he took on the job of delivering them to Morven Hills in the Lindis Pass. He must have done this well, because he was immediately engaged as a boundary rider and later became head shepherd on the station.

Once John was established in his new life, he sailed back to Scotland on a cattle boat to court an old friend, Christina Ross. He must have been well received as Christina came out to New Zealand in 1866 and married John in Christchurch the following year. From here they travelled to Morven Hills and set up house in a solitary shepherd's hut by a tussock-covered ravine on the outskirts of the station. Built of stone with a corrugated-iron roof, this single-roomed dwelling had no ceiling or insulation. It would have been grim at any time of year, but was especially so in winter. Cooking was done on a coal or wooden range, plumbing would have been entirely non-existent and furniture very basic.

Christina's life must have been lonely in that isolated spot. Other than her husband John, the only company to be had was that of passing shepherds, and she would hardly ever have seen another woman. The loneliness would have been intense. Self-sufficiency was an essential, as practically everything had to be carried in on horseback or by slow-moving bullock wagon. When shortages occurred it could be a long time before new supplies could be obtained. It helped to have a small garden with potatoes, some vegetables, gooseberries, elderberries and maybe a patch of oats for porridge and the horses. The mail that occasionally arrived by packhorse at Morven Hills probably sat there for a while before it eventually found its way to the outlying huts.

It was all but impossible to get medical help, so when there was sickness there was little option but to try old home remedies. The local midwife, Mrs Small of Lagoon Valley, rode over and helped when the Polsons' first child, Roderick, was born, and it's possible that she was booked for the delivery of Christina's twins, expected in 1869. However, there'd have been no way of contacting her when Christina went into premature labour. In later years John and Christina's grandson, the Reverend Ian Polson, wrote:

> . . . the two little mites were born not only without the last-minute preparations, but also in the midst of a severe winter with a heavy fall of snow round the hut. No doctor, nurse or neighbour could be called and Grandfather Polson took the two babes on his knees and kept them warm by the fire, while Grandma attended to herself as best she could. But the cold and the prematurity of the birth, plus the Spartan conditions, were too much for the twins and first one died and then the other. The snow was too deep for the police to come from Cromwell to examine them and indeed it was scarcely possible to bury them for the ground was frozen hard and deep.

Christina must have been devastated. I am sure she wanted them close, but out of sight, and that is how it is — John buried them on a sunny slope one gully over, about a half hour's walk from their cottage. He planted a willow stick to mark the spot. When I first came to Morven Hills in 1954 the stick had grown into a full-blown willow with a large, flat, grey stone entwined in the roots. I could still see the date, 1869, clearly etched on the stone.

Wild weather

My mother was always quoting stories of the devastating losses Morven Hills suffered in the early days. In 1895, almost all of Morven Hills was blanketed with snow and 37,000 sheep were lost.

IN 1903 THOUSANDS of sheep died after a heavy fall of snow lay over much of the station for some weeks. In all, 27,875 sheep were lost. Dray-loads of frozen carcasses brought in from the surrounding countryside were piled up in the paddock opposite the Tarras School to be burnt. Whenever possible the skins were removed and sold to help offset the massive loss.

Wild weather wasn't only the subject of tales from an earlier time. On 4 November 1981 we had a terrific storm. There were gale-force winds all day; no telephone and no electricity. At 10.40 p.m. we were asleep in our beds when we were awoken by a plaintive voice in the hall calling, 'Max . . .' It was Cliff. He told us that the old house had lost part of the roof over the living room and he was frightened that the entire roof would be whipped off. Max and Richard got dressed and went down to render assistance, as did Doug Still, who had come up for the weekend. They threw ropes over the roof and battened it down as best they could. However, the wind was so ferocious that this took nearly two hours. I was very nervous on my own and was so worried that the windows would blow in that I put my head under the blankets and bit my nails. The three Stills spent the night in our house and eventually the wind eased and was replaced by heavy rain. Next morning everything was as calm as a millpond but the place was littered with debris. Cliff's henhouse had been blown over and three hens squashed; he also lost a dog when a branch came down on the kennel. However, the woolshed and the shearers' quarters remained intact.

As long as I had been at Morven Hills we had always had a swingbridge over the Lindis River just down from the old cookshop. The original I remember was a single plank between two wire supports and was fun to walk over. In the middle of May 1982 we had over 12 centimetres of rain in one week. The Lindis flooded and swept away the bridge.

Some five months later, in October, Linda Still and her husband Donald Bates came home on holiday with their baby, Jason. Donald had been in the military and he asked Max if he could build a new bridge, a technique he had learnt in the army. Max was pleased, ordered the wood, and in a week Donald had a new bridge across the Lindis. I regret I don't have any photos but it was a masterpiece, and such a clever piece of engineering. Max was thrilled. Mother happened to be staying and he insisted on driving us down and asking Mother to be the first to walk across it. It was duly named Bates's Bridge.

A winter scene at Morven Hills.

A country wedding

On 6 January 1976, Bronwyn began her nursing career at the Christchurch Public Hospital, boarding in the Hagley nurses' home.

THIS WAS TO HAVE a sequel 12 months later when she rang home and said she wasn't enjoying it and thought she would give it up. She sounded so despondent living in the nurses' home that we bought a flat in Hereford Street and she moved in there. That was much better, and on 20 September 1979, we went to Christchurch for Bronwyn's graduation. Doctor Fairgray gave the graduation address. He told the nurses to never forget the five important bones: the wishbone, the jawbone, the knucklebone, the funny bone and finally the most important of all, the backbone, of which they must have plenty. He was very impressive.

The day after the graduation Bronwyn announced her

engagement to Peter Kerr. The couple had met when he was studying at Lincoln. They set their wedding for Saturday, 19 January 1980 and asked if they could be married at home in the woolshed. The next two months were taken up with wedding arrangements such as choosing frocks, planning the service and sending out invitations. We were all in a flood of excitement.

At the end of October I made the wedding cake. It was a pound mixture with eight eggs and five pounds of fruit soaked in one cup of brandy overnight. It looked fine, but with fruit cakes, you never know how good they are until you make the first cut. The following week I baked a second wedding cake just to make sure there was enough for everyone to have a piece. When we asked the Reverend Bernard Wilkinson, who had been the vicar at Cromwell in the early years, to take the service he was rather stunned to hear that the wedding was going to be held in the woolshed. He said he would need to get special dispensation from the bishop, which he duly did.

The men got to work, cleaned out the woolshed and then scrubbed all the wood in the wool storage area where the actual ceremony was to take place. They ringed this area with bales of wool that Max had held back after shearing, then cut a swathe of grass from the shed to the house for the guests to walk across. I'd suggested to Max that we should order a marquee but he was adamant it wasn't necessary.

We asked the Presbyterian Church in Tarras if we could 'borrow' the Polson organ as the Polsons had lived and worked at Morven Hills for many years. We also arranged to use the silver cross that Mother had bought for the Anglican church on our trip to London. When the boys drove down to Tarras to pick up the organ and cross, they also collected chairs from the Tarras hall.

We cleaned and scrubbed the shearers' quarters and turned them into motels. Eric, who had arrived for his usual summer holiday, put his hand up to be Commander-in-Chief. He was in his element. He took up residence in the cook's bedroom, and remained there for eight days prior to, during and after the wedding, dispensing cooked breakfasts (bacon and eggs) as well as morning, afternoon and late-night teas for any guest who didn't fit into the homestead — up to 10 at any time. At lunch and dinner times they came across to me.

Eric and Richard drove to Dunedin to pick up the alcohol. The food was very simple: ham and turkey with salads and new potatoes set out on tables in the carport. Dessert came in the form of huge bowls of raspberries from Waimate, served with homemade pavlovas. I asked Mrs Craig from Cromwell to help with the preparation and presentation. I was determined to have flowers so engaged a Timaru florist, Pat Richards. I wanted pink carnations so Pat ordered them from Auckland and then made six glorious standard carnation trees to line the aisle in the shed. The flowers looked terrific, but so they should have as they cost more than the food.

On the big day, it rained steadily all morning. The forecast was gloomy and it was still raining until 11 a.m. when, as if by a miracle, the skies cleared and warm sunshine lifted the day. Unfortunately the wind got stronger and colder as the day wore on and the overall impression was of a cold, miserable, windy day. Yet, strangely, the sun occasionally peeped through. Bronwyn looked lovely in a calf-length cream crêpe frock and her bridesmaid, Sarah Scott, wore a similar frock of duck-egg blue. Tarras friend Sue Young played the organ as everyone sang 'Praise my soul the King of Heaven' and 'Now thank we all our God' at full volume. The acoustics were amazing. As the happy couple signed the register on a wool bale, the sun shone down on them through a dormer window as Sue played 'Somewhere, My Love' from *Dr Zhivago*, giving me a lovely tingling down the spine. The entire service had such great reverence that you couldn't help but be moved.

After the service the men loaded the piano on the Land Rover and took it over to the woolshed. Then, once the pianist arrived, we had a good old-fashioned barn dance.

It was such a relief to have the day over, after all the planning. There was only one casualty. Two days later, in the storeroom, we found a huge tray of sliced salmon and lemon on what had once been fresh bread. Irma and Ken

Andrews had made it, but Ken had slipped it in and then forgot to tell anyone. The hens thought it was Christmas.

After their honeymoon, the newlyweds moved to Hamilton, Bronwyn to nurse in the hospital and Peter to do contract fencing. A couple of years later, on 27 March 1983, Tom Cowie rang and asked if Peter and Bronwyn were interested in the position of married couple at 'Clearvue', a farmstead in Central Otago. The four of us were invited down for afternoon tea to discuss the proposition. After a week's thought Bronwyn and Peter decided to take the position, and they began work on 18 April 1983.

Christmas Cake

(used for Bronwyn's wedding cake)

1½ lb (680 grams) sultanas
1 lb (450 grams) currants
½ lb (225 grams) seeded raisins
¼ lb (115 grams) cherries
6 oz (170 grams) almonds
2 oz (60 grams) peel
2 tablespoons marmalade
1 cup rum
rind and juice of 1 lemon
rind and juice of 1 orange
1 lb (450 grams) butter
1 lb (450 grams) sugar
1¼ lb (570 grams) flour
¼ teaspoon baking powder
8 eggs
pinch of salt

Prepare fruit and leave covered with rum and juices overnight. Mix everything together and bake for six hours at 300°F (150°C).

My annus horribilis

The boys had both gone off to do their OE in the early 1980s. Both travelled extensively and both were gone for some time. We were glad that they had their youthful adventures, but their return was always something special.

ON 25 NOVEMBER 1982, at precisely 8.30 p.m., Richard arrived home from his big OE, moustached, weary and 6 kilograms lighter after travelling through India and Nepal. Peter had driven to Christchurch to meet him. There was great excitement and we all wanted to talk and ask questions at the same time. Bronwyn and Peter arrived a few days after this, having stopped off in Timaru. All the family were back in the nest.

I've never forgotten the day Peter came home. On Sunday 16 October 1983, I was writing letters at the kitchen table when

I noticed a dark head bob by the window. I was amazed when Peter walked in the door, unannounced. He had been in England for seven months and, tired of the dismal weather, had decided to cash in his return ticket, flown to Auckland, down to Christchurch, stayed the night in the flat and then caught the Mt Cook bus down next day. He left his luggage at the gate and walked up the drive. It was such a surprise. Max and Richard were equally surprised, and happy to have an extra pair of hands with mustering and shearing round the corner. We had a glass of wine with our dinner that night.

Those were happy days. Little could we have guessed how things would change a few years later.

On Tuesday 19 March 1985, cattle were going away to the works and the men were away early to get them into the yards. Because it was on her side of the river, I knew Doreen would be giving them morning tea and all would be well. The boys were always telling me Doreen made the nicer biscuits, which they called 'Cliff's Favourites'. It was a standing joke. Sometimes I used her recipe but my biscuits never tasted like hers.

When the cattle were being loaded one unruly beast kicked out in fury, the steel door swung back and the steel D-lug that went over the clip hit Max on the temple. He staggered and fell to the ground, bleeding profusely. He insisted that there was nothing the matter but I wrapped a crêpe bandage round his head, and Peter took him to Cromwell to see the doctor, a 60-kilometre drive. He was duly bandaged and was back for dinner, which he didn't want. His head was throbbing and he started to hallucinate, saying the weirdest things. When he didn't recognise Richard it was obvious that things weren't right, so off we went to Cromwell again.

This time the doctor took one look at Max and had him admitted to the Cromwell hospital, where an x-ray revealed a fractured skull. Max was promptly put on a plane to Dunedin. When I arrived at Dunedin Hospital the next morning Max was propped up in bed, his head had been shaved and he had an enormous scar from one ear to the other. 'Eat your heart out Yul Brynner,' I said. Although alert, he was very confused.

He thought he was still in Cromwell; in fact he told me he could see the large Wellingtonian pines that were a feature of the landscape there.

When Max was in hospital I boarded in the nurses' home, and spent most of my time sitting in the ward. At times he'd hallucinate about the visitors he thought had called to see him. Every day he told me Jock Dougherty, the Oamaru wool buyer, had come in and wanted to buy the Morven Hills wool clip. I asked the nurse if this was true and she said no. The physiotherapists then found him a little notebook and insisted he write down everything that unfolded during the day. From that moment on until the end of his life he was never without a notebook, and he never bought a shirt without a pocket.

At the beginning of the third week, Mr Christie, the neurosurgeon, walked in. He told me that Max had made amazing progress, and it was probably due to his physical fitness prior to the accident, and that he wasn't a smoker. He continued, 'I'm ready to discharge him, providing he abides by a few set rules. He has to take a break from farming for six months, no stress, no physical work, no lifting, no driving until he comes off his medication in a year, no alcohol for the same period and no sex.' Max leaned back on the pillow and said, 'Just shoot me.' Mr Christie replied, 'Please yourself.' By this stage his hair was growing out and the scar was less prominent. The following day he was discharged and we drove home. He loved being among the hills again and continued to gain strength, pottering round doing odd jobs, but he was less social than before the accident.

Disaster struck again just three months later. The phone rang as we were about to have our evening meal on 15 June 1985. It was Doreen, talking in a whisper, as though she was frightened someone was eavesdropping. 'There's been an accident. I think you should come down, but don't bring Max.' John Patterson, our neighbour at Bargour, had been using his bulldozer to clean up the willows by the river when he was knocked off the seat by a branch and then run over by the bulldozer. It was dark and after 7 p.m. as I drove down the Morven Hills flat and up the Bargour drive. The dogs went crazy and were barking for all their worth so I didn't have to knock. A little boy opened the door and said, 'Where's my dad?' I found John's wife, Carol, and her mother seated round a welcoming fire. I said I was very sorry to intrude, but there had been a dreadful accident. When Carol's mother asked if John had been killed, I replied, 'Yes.' She asked lots of questions, but Carol was so shocked and stunned that she never once opened her mouth. I cried all the way home; it was the hardest thing I ever had to do. It was too sad for words. John was 35, in the prime of his life.

Things got much worse a few weeks later. On Saturday 20 July, the phone rang at 1.45 a.m. It was Bronwyn, telling us there had been a car accident at the junction of Fendalton Road and Harper Avenue in Christchurch, and that Peter had been admitted to intensive care. As the three of us stood in the kitchen struck dumb, Richard said, 'I'll drive you up in the morning.' I sat down in the hall with my back to the wall and wept copiously. Max tousled my hair and said, 'Come on, old girl, everything will be fine,' but I said emphatically, 'No, our lives will never be the same.'

It turned out that Peter and his class had been drinking at a Lincoln pub after sitting exams. He then gave his car keys to a friend who was unfamiliar with the car. Peter was sitting in the back without a seatbelt when the car skidded off the road and hit an oak tree, right where Peter was sitting. The two in the front seats were unhurt, but Peter suffered serious head injuries, including a fractured skull. I don't blame anyone; it was just one of those strange quirks of life where you put it behind you and get on with living.

During the next heartbreaking six weeks I visited Peter every day at the hospital. Family friend Roberta Goodger, who worked in the heart ward, called to see Peter every morning before she went on duty. She was absolutely brilliant — she'd bring Peter food like whitebait patties which she thought he would like for breakfast. The phone rang continually, food and flowers kept appearing. I couldn't believe the kindness of friends. Bronwyn spent time talking to Peter, trying to stimulate him with news of Morven Hills, how we were advertising for a new musterer, and she felt sure he mouthed the word 'sheep'.

On the day that neurosurgeon Mr McFarlane told me that Peter was likely to need care all his life I was crying in the cafeteria when the Catholic chaplain, Sister Patricia Clark, pulled her chair close to mine, put her arm round my shoulders and said, 'Never give up hope, the doctors aren't always right.' She continued, 'Live one day at a time and don't think about the future.' And then she told me to eat my macaroni cheese before it got cold. When I stood up to go back to the ward, she said, 'Remember, God never gives you more than what you can cope with.'

Max was also devastated — he had planned for Richard and Peter to farm Morven Hills together. The station was easily big enough to be run by the two brothers, but after Peter's accident it soon became clear that wasn't a possibility. Coming only a few months after his own injury, it was a lot of stress for Max to manage.

Two days later I drove back to Central Otago. It was a Friday and Bronwyn's daughter Sarah was being christened on the Sunday. We were getting ready for church when the phone rang. I answered it and a voice at the end of the line said, 'How ya doing?' It was Peter. I asked him what had happened and he said he'd had a big sleep and just woken up. That morning he had said to the nurse, 'I want to ring my parents and this is their phone number.' It was 8 September, six weeks after the accident, and that was the first time we knew his brain was functioning. Things were looking up.

Mr McFarlane told us Peter would need physiotherapy, speech therapy and several eye operations but, providing we had a housekeeper for him, he could stay at the flat and the hospital would send a van each day to pick him up. Friends had been so generous with food and flowers, get-well cards, letters and visits that I decided to send a thank-you letter. After explaining that Peter's recovery would take at least two years, I wrote:

During the past fourteen weeks we have been supported by the kindness of many people. The phone calls, baking, letters, cards, telegrams and beautiful flowers have given us strength to face each day. Although nothing was acknowledged at the time, we want you to know we greatly appreciate all your kind actions and thoughts.

We count our blessings when we think of friends like you.

Thank you.
Madge and Max.

I had 100 copies printed and I posted a copy to everyone who had got in touch, sent get-well cards, phoned, called, or dropped in food or flowers. When Eric received this letter he rang from England and said, 'Don't advertise for a housekeeper.' He insisted, 'I will fly out and look after Peter.' It was a marvellous offer and he flew out just as soon as he could. Once he arrived we gave Eric money in order to buy whatever was required. He kept a detailed account of every cent he spent, washed and ironed and was as good as any woman. The hospital sent a van Monday to Friday and Peter continued having all the treatment he needed with physiotherapists and speech therapists. Unfortunately, Peter's life did a U-turn after this accident, and he has had to cope with a raft of health problems.

RICHARD HAD BEEN COURTING Anne McElroy for some years when they announced their engagement in 1985. Once they were engaged, the pressure was on to find a place for them to live. I was taken aback when Max suggested building a Lockwood house on the farm, as all his life he was very careful with money. Max kept a tight rein on the finances and we often went without things that he said weren't essential. If it didn't benefit the farm, it was unnecessary. At one stage the boys were very keen to buy a boat, but Max said, 'Over my dead body.' And remember the tennis court? We only got that because I paid the bill. These were unimportant items; quite different to posts, fencing and superphosphate which would improve the property. Max was a bit like my mother who, having lived through the Depression, had a catch cry of 'Can you live without it?' If you answered in the affirmative she always said, 'Well, don't buy it.' We never went without. It's just that Max was very careful.

Once we'd chosen a Lockwood house we had to decide where it was to go. After much discussion we settled on a mound of land below the shearing shed. Although this was dry and barren, it had wonderful vistas both down and up the valley. I often wished we'd put our homestead there. Once the decision had been made, we were surprised how quickly the house went up. There was still a lot of worry about Peter's health so a large wedding celebration wasn't appropriate. Anne and Richard were married in a small, quiet ceremony in the Oamaru Gardens on 23 December 1985. Archdeacon Bernard Wilkinson officiated and the only people there were the two families, my brother Bill, his wife Frances and Eric.

Peter had another month of therapy in Christchurch but at the end of January the physios and therapists considered he'd made sufficient progress to be able to return home. The neurosurgeon Mr McFarlane told us not to take Peter away from his home environment for two years as that would be too confusing for him. Mr Suckling operated on his eyes in February, the first of five operations.

Anne and Richard had set up home in the cookshop, so now that the Lockwood was up and running, Peter moved in there and Ken Fairweather, an ex-station cook from Nokamai Station in Southland, moved in as housekeeper. It would have been impossible to find anyone more congenial.

At around this time, we also lost a Morven Hills identity. One day when Max made his daily visit to check on George

Martin he found him dead on the floor. He tried to get in touch with relations but after ringing all round, it appeared no one wanted to claim him. However, he was a Great War veteran, so the Returned Services took over and he is buried in the Cromwell cemetery. It was the end of an era when George passed away.

While all this was going on, there were good things as well. It was wonderful to have a growing family.

The year 1984 had started well when, on the very first day, Peter Kerr rang to say we had a granddaughter. I was so excited that I felt as though God had leaned over and dropped a garland on my head. We drove to Cromwell to see Bronwyn and the baby, Nicola Jane. We thought she looked very much like her father. About 18 months later, on 4 June 1985, Bronwyn produced another daughter, Sarah Louise — a little star to brighten our year. I felt as if another garland had fallen on my head.

Our grandchildren count doubled when Richard's wife Anne presented us with twins, Hamish and Amanda Snow, born in Oamaru in November 1988. And a year later, Andrew Kerr popped out, followed by Angus Kerr in 1991. He was the full stop in that family. Two of each, how blessed they were. William Snow filled the bassinette at Morven Hills on 26 July 1993, bringing the total grandchildren to seven. He came out smiling, and has smiled ever since.

top
Bronwyn at her graduation.

bottom
Max reading *New Zealand Farmer*.

LEAVING
MORVEN
HILLS

Changing of the guard

The threads of life are numerous and far-reaching. We may tangle them or break them, arrange them roughly or meticulously, tie ourselves in knots or weave without a wobble, but the design is not without meaning, colour or productivity.

THIRTY-THREE ACTION-PACKED YEARS went into the rich tapestry of our life at Morven Hills, and I would like to think we left behind a picture that the next generation can pick up, run with and improve on. The time had come when it was necessary to step aside. So at Labour Weekend 1987, it was time to pack up and say a sad farewell to Morven and the hills we both loved so much. Anne and Richard moved into the homestead.

Some years earlier, Max and I had been thinking of buying a piece of land in Wanaka with an eye on retirement, and a section with a cottage had become available on Beacon Point Road. Back we went. Max wasn't that keen, but I thought it had potential. Arthur and Bernice Barnett were asking $110,000 and we took possession on 28 March 1983.

We soon realised that the cottage was impossible to enlarge and that we would be better to save our money and put it towards a new house. In 1985 the phone rang one morning and it was Ken Smith; not long after we'd taken possession of the Wanaka cottage we'd got in touch with him regarding the building of a new home. He asked what we had in mind and we said a lounge of a similar size to the farm one, a big kitchen, two en suite bedrooms (one with a bath and the other with a shower), a large office and a double garage with a walk-in cool room. I asked that it all be on one level, no steps, and because we enjoyed entertaining, nice private areas.

We didn't have an architect. Together the three of us came up with an acceptable plan. I originally put the garage in the back corner with the door leading through to the laundry but when Ken looked at the plan, he said, 'Cars will park out in front. Why don't you bring the garage forward so that you get a sheltered, private area?' He was quite right.

By the time Ken was ready to make a start, Max was in hospital after his accident. Ken was anxious to get going because his gang were waiting, but where to put the house? I drove over and together Ken and I walked all over the section. If the house was sited down by the road, there'd be a grand view of the lake, but Ken said the traffic would be much too noisy. We decided not to put the house at the back of the section as it would be too close to the cottage. In the end the middle seemed right. I knew I wanted to have two lots of concrete washing tubs for my small bulbs, so allowance was made for them on the southern boundary. By the time Max was discharged from hospital the builders were well underway.

Not long after we moved to Wanaka, Mother rang to say she didn't think she could manage on her own much longer and thought it was time she came and lived with us. Mother settled in well in the cottage, my brother Bill and Frances came along regularly to see her and she was very happy. She loved to put on her old straw hat and walk around the garden, so we had seats strategically placed so she could sit down and admire the view. Each Sunday night we went to Barrow's Tavern for a treat, and we all took turns at paying. On some Sundays she insisted Max drive her car because she said it needed a run.

In May 1989 we bought Peter a small farm at Omakau, between Alexandra and Ranfurly. It was all flat and it was hoped he would be able to manage it. The house was deplorable but Ken Smith, our 'Mr Fixit', came to the rescue again. He and his men took out walls, turned the kitchen round, put in a dishwasher, built a new shower and made it much more liveable. Max sometimes drove the men down in his Lada and spent a week helping. His Russian vehicle took a lot of flak from the men. Bronwyn, who lived nearby, was wonderful. She has always been a good provider and has excellent organisational skills. Even with three small children she gave the builders a cooked meal at night. Peter called his farm 'Nevrom Downs', which is Morven spelt backwards.

Many hard years followed. Although Peter was bright when he first came home, his recovery was sporadic. Sometimes it went well, at other times things were very tough. Fortunately he enjoyed overseas trips and occasional relationships gave some balance to his life. In 2008 a Southland dairy farmer made Peter an offer he couldn't refuse for his little farm and he moved to Wanaka. He now lives permanently in the cottage, which I really enjoy as he comes down and has dinner with me each night, except at the weekends. I enjoy cooking for him, and he makes sure I have more than tea and toast for dinner!

Peter's a nice man with an easy, outgoing personality. Life has dealt him a dud hand, but he always looks on the bright side and is a pleasure to have in the house. As they say, life is not about waiting for the storm to pass, it's about learning to dance in the rain.

A new garden beckons

When we bought the Wanaka property, I set about creating a garden. The Barnetts had planted a *Photinia* hedge around the cottage, which was one of the first things we got rid of.

A BLUEGUM WHICH ARTHUR BARNETT had carried up from Dunedin in the boot of his car and planted directly in front of the cottage was also destined to have a short life. Like the proverbial beanstalk, in a few short years it had shot up. Every time Max cut the lawn he had to spend the first half hour gathering up the bark and the rubbish. He said it had to go. When friends Rosemary and Ross Kerr were here for a few days, Ross volunteered to be the executioner. Out came the chainsaw and down it came. Max smiled all day.

It was fun watching the garden develop from a bare paddock. It takes about six years before you begin to see the first layer, then it matures very quickly. After that, you are cutting back.

My first love is trees, especially maples. We go through certain stages in the gardening cycle. At Morven Hills it was irises and small bulbs and I was a member of the Scottish Rock Garden Society. Although I brought several of the good irises with me, they haven't done as well as they did in the hot, dry Lindis. Roses, on the other hand, were an early standout. I planted both courtyards with hybrid tea roses and had a love affair with them for several years. But after 10 years or so, they grew old and woody so I got Rod Key to dig them all out. Now I'm crazy about hydrangeas and marvel at how easy they are to grow with so little attention. Raspberry Crush is a firm favourite.

During the summer months Max and I always worked feverishly in the garden. I'd buy the plants and Max would plant them. Nearly everything in my Wanaka garden is named. Whenever I purchase a plant or tree, I bring it into the office and then record it on the computer before I plant it. I've done this for 25 years, so when I look at my lists I know exactly how old plants are and where they've come from. I am fanatical about names. I hate spending a lot of money and then in a few years not being sure what it is that I have.

After one trip away we returned to find that all our newly planted camellia trees had been ring-barked by the rabbits. All we were left with were stumps, without one piece of green bark showing. That gave us the idea to put tyres round the next planting to protect them from these furry critters. Rabbits do enormous damage. I have planted crocus by the thousands but every spring they mow them off like a lawn mower. I suspect they look upon them as an aphrodisiac.

One year on a visit to England I was so smitten with heathers that I bought a book on them by Valerie Proudley. I wanted to plant something along the front of our Wanaka section that was low-growing and yet colourful, and heathers appeared to fit the bill. After I arranged to buy 500 at $4.55 each I did a trade with Max. He said, 'If you pay for the plants, I will dig the holes.' We shook hands, it was a deal. The soil was very sandy so the digging wasn't that difficult, but first I bought 24 bales of pea straw and mulched the ground. I didn't go overseas that year, just a trip round the section with a big buy-up of plants. I was so delighted with the heathers that we drove all over the South Island looking for different varieties and then planted another four beds. Apart from November, when the winter ones have finished flowering and the summer ones are yet to flower, there is colour for 11 months of the year and, better still, they suppress the weeds.

I have always been passionate about daffodils. Through trial and error, I have discovered the further south you purchase them, the better they do, so I've bought most of mine from Maple Glen nursery in Southland. After I joined the New Zealand Daffodil Society in September 2012, Bronwyn drove me to Dunedin for the World Daffodil Convention. It was fabulous, though I have to be honest and say I have no enthusiasm for pink-cupped daffodils.

When we bought the land in Wanaka in 1983 there wasn't a house to be seen from our place, but by 1992 the town was spreading closer and closer like an uncontrollable rash. Max called Willy Rankin and asked him to top the pines and clear the back section. The plantation of pines on our northern boundary meant that half our section was enveloped in shade. Up until the time we moved to Wanaka I hadn't grown camellias and rhododendrons as the Lindis was much too dry for them. But then I had the bright idea that if I could water them properly, they would do well in the shady area. I bought several trailer-loads from Ken Jordan's Nurseries in Ashburton and we planted them up and down in the shaded areas. However, no sooner had we finished planting them when all the pines were cleared, leaving my precious plants sitting in full sun. Fortunately they have acclimatised and despite the occasional ferocious wind are doing well some 20 years later. Each year I plant all my surplus bulbs in the top area as well.

By the time we'd been in Wanaka for a few years the main garden was creeping further up the back. Every autumn we made a new planting, and eventually the garden reached beyond the cottage. I haunted garden centres looking for different maples so that I could build up a collection. I would rather have a new maple than a new car. On the north side our neighbours had a pine hedge, and although it sucked all the goodness out of the soil, it provided wonderful protection for the maple trees. They also kept it well trimmed, which was a bonus.

MOTHER WAS HAPPILY SETTLED in the cottage but grew a little frailer with every passing month. Most evenings Max would drive up and bring her down to the main house, and then drive her back after dinner. One July she said, 'You know the cottage doesn't get much sun at this time of the year.' When the sun was low in the winter sky the plantations of Douglas firs on the adjacent land blocked it out. She suggested we should contact Fraser Urquhart, who owned the farm, with the idea of buying a small piece. When I wrote a letter to Mr Urquhart explaining the problem he and his wife Ivy agreed to sell us the adjoining land. Suddenly we were the proud owners of 1.6 hectares overlooking Lake Wanaka, not far from the middle of town. We were ecstatic.

Mother's health was showing signs of coming to the end of the road. In the late spring she complained of pains in her chest and she was admitted to Dunedin Hospital soon after. When she was discharged, shortly after Christmas, Max and I went down, loaded up with blankets and pillows ready to make a bed up in the back seat. She came out in a wheelchair and I was sad to see how frail she was. We had her in our spare bedroom where we could keep an eye on her. On the night of 3 January 1993 I asked her what she felt like and she said stewed tomatoes on toast. When I took them in she asked, 'Did you remember to put a pinch of sugar with them?' I had to smile; even on her deathbed she was teaching me how to cook. She died the next day. She was buried on Wednesday 6 January, in her ninetieth year.

The Wanaka house and garden.

In 1993 the breast-screening bus was here in Wanaka and I thought I'd better do the right thing and make an appointment. Taken by surprise, I got a recall from Dunedin Hospital; they wanted me to have another x-ray, as there was a blip on the film and it needed investigating. It didn't concern me greatly. My health was excellent, I was playing golf, gardening and I'd never felt better. I was diagnosed with breast cancer and on 3 June 1993 I underwent a mastectomy.

To make the trips to Dunedin Hospital more palatable, each time we went down Max did a detour via Balclutha to see Heather Metherell at her Southwell Nursery at Hillend. Heather was always so bright and bubbly that she made us feel good. In those days most plants sold for $2.80 and we always loaded the boot up. This wasn't the only time we went on plant-buying sprees. Every spring Max and I had a night in Gore, and a day at Bob and Muriel Davison's Maple Glen, my favourite garden in the South Island. This was a shot in the arm for any gardener. Every time we went there a fence (or fences) had been extended and there was a new piece of garden flourishing under Muriel's guidance. Her foresight and energy took my breath away. I salute her vision.

Retirement had a lovely ring to it. We loved the freedom of Wanaka. In May 1994 Tony Anderson walked across the road with the plan of Atherton Place, the new subdivision which he had been developing directly in front of our house. I had asked him if he could give us first choice when they were ready to go on the market. So here he was, the lovely man, with seven sections to choose from. He said, 'Take your pick. They are all the same price: two hundred thousand dollars.' We chose number 2 Atherton Place, directly opposite us, in order to protect our lake view. As an added bonus, it has a right of way beside sections 4 and 6, down to the lake, which adds to the area that can't be built upon.

Cliff and Doreen Still retired a year after us and built a new home in Tarras. They had been wonderful employees, and to have spent 31 years with us was beyond the call of duty. It was always a harmonious relationship and we operated like one big, happy family. Cliff was very hard-working, as was

Doreen. When Cliff left Morven Hills in 1988, his wheel turned full circle as he became general factotum at Malvern Downs. He had begun work there on 2 January 1948, then spent the next 31 years at Morven Hills, and he was now back at Malvern Downs. In all he chalked up a good 60 years of service to the Gibson family. Mother would have been so proud of him.

Max and I continued enlarging the garden, and spring, summer and autumn days were always spent planning, planting, maintaining and developing our Wanaka plot. Gardening has great therapeutic powers. I was anti-native and anti-conifer so purchased only deciduous trees. I felt very strongly that we should be planting for colour in Central Otago. Maples were good and rowans gave a double bonus as they had berries as well as beautiful hues. We engaged American Bill Gibson to establish the watering system and from then on he was a constant visitor to our property. 'Visitor' is hardly the right word; 'labourer' I should say. I'd call him 'Mr Let's-put-it-this-way'. I couldn't have done without him. We opened the garden to the public 10 a.m. to 4 p.m. and made a charge of $5. It gave me such pleasure and I felt it was a shame not to share it with like-minded gardeners. Unfortunately it is now closed.

The Kerr grandchildren's playhouse was turned into a henhouse, which was put at the back of the section (which Max called his 'high country'). Peter Kerr fenced a run to give the hens plenty of space. Once a year we drove down to McLean's Poultry Farm at Roxburgh East and bought 12 red shaver hens. Max diligently looked after them morning and night, and had a clientele for fresh eggs which he usually delivered.

During 2008 an Alexandra man, John Sutton, and his son Andrew had been staying in the cottage while they put the Millennium Track round the lake. When that was finished and they were preparing to take their gear home, John asked me if I would like him to make a trench on the property. I could have kissed him; it was an offer too good to refuse. He dug the trench in the top block and we planted 1000 daffodil bulbs.

I would also like to pay tribute to Lyn Key who has been with me for 14 years and who gives me two full-on hours in the garden every week, usually on a Friday. She has been truly amazing. Between us, we have kept it looking reasonably tidy, but progressively she is doing more and I am doing less. Peter cuts the lawns.

top
Looking down from the back garden, with Lake Wanaka and Mt Roy in the background.

bottom
Cliff and Doreen Still, who worked with us at Morven Hills for over 30 years, in 2012.

Full circle

By the early 2000s Max had real heart problems and was taking all kinds of medication to counteract them. Always busy, he had joined the Probus club and was also active in St Columba's Anglican church.

IN THOSE DAYS WE had a box number at the post office and Max loved going to pick up the mail and chatting to farmers of his vintage. However, his health continued to decline and in February 2003 he had a heart bypass operation in Christchurch. The next day was our forty-ninth wedding anniversary so I purchased a large helium balloon that said 'I love you' and tied it to the towel rail on Max's locker.

Although Max slowed down after the operation he was doing wonderfully well. He still walked up to feed his hens, morning and night, and he enjoyed raking the abundance of leaves. He found small jobs to undertake, but no digging. Probably after his operation his circulation wasn't so good and he felt the cold acutely. He definitely wasn't going to spend a winter in Wanaka. I suggested we go to Australia, but no, he had his heart set on Africa yet again . . . (We had visited South Africa eight times by then.)

Max died on Sunday 30 June 2008, on Richard's birthday. We had a very simple, brief ceremony, just as he wanted. Rosemary McVay arranged the greenery on his coffin after the grandchildren, Hamish and William, had gathered it off his beloved Morven Hills, and we placed a South African tie, which Brian Davies had given him, alongside. It was a fitting symbol because you seldom saw Max without a tie, and rugby was his great passion. He was 83. He had told us who he wanted as his pallbearers; he particularly wanted Cliff Still. After all, they had worked together for over 30 years.

I describe that period in my life as being akin to an eclipse; the sun disappeared and my world turned grey. But I knew it was only a matter of time until the sun would reappear. After all, there are people all over the world who never see it at all.

In July 2008 I had three weeks in Coolangatta. I didn't feel well. I had no energy and everything was such an effort. It was like pushing a wheelbarrow uphill. Back in Wanaka I made an appointment to have the pacemaker that I'd had fitted in 2000 checked at Dunedin Hospital at the end of August. It quickly became apparent the battery in my pacemaker was dead. It was meant to go through until November but had stopped the first week of July. The doctors were appalled, said I shouldn't be walking round, and wondered how I had managed. I told them, I hadn't. They bundled me straight into hospital. The old battery was replaced on Monday morning. I picked up instantly and felt a new woman. This new battery is supposed to last 10 years.

Once I had my new pacemaker fitted I was feeling so much better that travel beckoned. Before the end of the year, in October, I flew off to the States, purposely to see the fall colours on the East Coast.

Max had asked for his ashes to be scattered in the house

paddock overlooking the homestead at Morven Hills. He specified the exact rock he stood on when he mustered the block; it had commanding views up and down the valley, in tune with the birds and the bleating of sheep. So on Christmas Day 2008 Richard's wife Anne cooked a fantastic Christmas family dinner and we then all trooped up the hill to the stone. To be honest it was jolly steep and they chauffeured me in the Land Rover while the young took their motorbikes. We sat the box on the stone and then, one by one, grandchildren and all, we took a small scoop and flung the ash to the four winds just as he wanted us to do. I thought back to when we had stopped on the top of the Lindis, newly married, full of hope and dreams and with a lone hawk drawing circles in the sky. Where had the years gone?

Now, 59 years on from that day at the top of the Lindis, the tree of life has a different shape. It has new branches and two of the old branches are dead. It has followed the constant pattern of removal and growth that all our lives follow. Things have passed, new things have come. I am surrounded by my family and grandchildren. In the circle of life, the latter are the seven new branches which will make the family tree strong again. Max was so proud of them. On the Kerr side, Nicola is a chef, Sarah a graphic artist, Andrew a civil engineer and Angus has completed a P.E. degree from Otago University. Of the Snows, Amanda is an architect, Hamish a pilot with Virgin Airlines and William is doing a course in avionics with the Air Force. I have two great-grandchildren, Finley and Pippa Kerr.

In 2012, Richard came over to Wanaka with a magnificent stone taken from where Max's ashes were scattered. He had a brass plaque mounted on it which reads:

R. M. Snow
17.7.1926 — 30.6.2008
A good shepherd

We have placed it under the copper beech tree which Max dug the hole for and helped to plant. Not many people see it, but I point it out when they come.

In the 27 years I have been here, Wanaka has swelled and burst like a ripe seed pod. New houses pop up every day. We have a dream library, magnificent medical and dental facilities and an assortment of restaurants, all ringed by my adored majestic mountains. There are numerous walking trails and I am very proud that, with the help of Nancy and Bob Parker, I managed to make it to the top of Mt Roy in February 1991, though coming down was difficult. Then in January 1997, along with Bronwyn and Peter Kerr and all the grandchildren, I walked to the top of the Rob Roy Glacier. That was very spectacular. I think it is the finest walk you can do here in Wanaka. Truthfully I couldn't think of a nicer place to live. Now I have a new companion — a walking stick.

My odometer clicked over at 83 in February. Family and friends are wonderful and I have them living close by. I've learned that it's not what I have in my life, but who I have in my life that counts. I count my blessings every day and think how lucky I am. Lyn and Rod Key have been my knights in shining armour: if something goes wrong, I ring Rod. And Richard is only a phone call away. He keeps an eye on me. So now I face a brave new world in slightly larger slacks, and wonder why they're using smaller print in the newspapers. At times the road has been pot-holed and rough, but it has been a wonderful journey.

top
Me with the grandchildren on the stone from which we scattered Max's ashes. Back: William, Hamish, Andrew, Sarah and Angus; front: Amanda. (Nicola was absent — in the Antarctic cooking on the *Spirit of Enderby*.)

bottom
Max and Nicola in the garden at Wanaka.

Image Credits

Douglas Badcock: paintings page 209 and page 1 of picture insert

Ruth Brown: pages 2–3, 8, 16–17, 18–19, 20, 34, 44, 56, 62, 70–71, 72, 80, 94, 104, 114–15, 116, 126, 134, 158, 168, 180, 209 (top), 210, 218–19, 220, 226, 230, 236, 246–47, 248, 252, 262 and all images in picture insert

Geoffrey P. Duff collection: pages 29, 33, 37, 49, 51, 54, 61, 129. From *Sheep May Safely Graze: A History of Morven Hills Station and the Tarras District* (self-published, 1978)

Madge Snow collection: pages 76, 78, 85, 91, 100, 109, 119, 123, 133, 137, 141, 145, 148, 153, 157, 161, 165, 166, 171, 176, 179, 187, 188, 191, 196, 205, 209, 217, 223, 229, 245, 256, 261, 267

Colin Wheeler: illustrations pages 5, 6–7, 11, 13. From *Historic Sheep Stations of the South Island* (Reed, 1968)

Every effort has been made to track down the copyright holders. If you have further information, please contact the publisher.